PREFACE

Trees are so familiar and commonplace that we often take them for granted. It is usually only when great changes affect the tree population, such as the aftermath of major storms or the rapid loss of thousands of trees from disease, that we realize what a major element they are in the world around us. In fact, few people live in entirely treeless surroundings, even in towns and cities, and trees have an important influence on everyday living, whether directly or indirectly.

Trees perform a number of vital functions in the environment. Like all green plants, they are able to use the energy of sunlight to manufacture basic foods, such as sugars, on which all life depends. As part of this process, they also help maintain the level of oxygen in the atmosphere. Trees play a significant role in preventing the erosion of soil by binding it with their roots, and their dead leaves greatly improve soil fertility when they rot to form humus. They also provide habitats for other wildlife, both animals and other plants, that rely on trees for food and shelter. Humans have always relied heavily on trees, and many species have important commercial uses. As well as timber for fuel and building, they yield food and drink, forage for domestic stock, and a variety of other products ranging from cork, paper pulp, matches, dyes, and tanning agents to perfumes, medicines, gums, and even jewellery. Nowadays, there is a large industry based solely on the use of trees as ornamental and amenity plants to delight the eye and improve the quality of our own, man-made, habitat.

HOW TO USE THIS BOOK

This book covers 170 species of trees, including all those commonly found in the wild in the United States, as well as those frequently planted in streets and public parks and gardens.

Each page of the main section of the book has a **photograph** of a tree, and an illustration showing additional details. The common name of the tree is given, together with its scientific name, and the name of the plant family to which it belongs. At the top of each page is an indication of the tree's height, and whether it is evergreen or deciduous. The lighter portion of the **calendar bar** indicates those months in which you will usually find this tree in flower. For conifers, the lighter portion indicates when the tree is shedding pollen from male cones (where this information is not available the calendar bar has been omitted). This is meant only as a guide. Flowering can be brought forward or delayed by several weeks, depending on the seasonal weather conditions. It can also be affected by geography—as a general rule flowering is delayed for trees growing further north.

The **ID Fact File** lists features that will help you to identify each species, and the general text provides further information.

To identify a tree, look through the book to find the most likely match. Use the ID Fact File to see if the description matches the tree. If it does not, check any similar trees described on adjacent pages. The species are arranged in order of their closest relationships, so the tree you are trying to identify should be nearby.

HISTORY OF TREES IN THE US

Geologically speaking, the story of trees in the United States begins with the last ice age, which radically altered established populations and distributions. Many species would have retreated south with the advancing ice, or migrated to the slopes and ridges of high mountain ranges. Once the ice began to retreat northward, some species recolonized their original northern range. Others took the opportunity to expand their range or, in some cases, stayed in the warmer, more favorable conditions in the south. For all species in North America, however, this period defines current distributions (discounting human influence).

Several main forest types became established at that time: coniferous pine and birch forests generally developed in the north, with more broadleaf forest types emerging in the south. In the warmer conditions of the extreme south, evergreen forests became more common. Mountain slopes were covered with spruce and fir forests while lowland swampy areas were readily colonized by species of willow and alder. Oaks colonized the major mountain ranges in the east and on the central plains.

Sixteenth-century European explorers would have found great swathes of cedar, poplar, and oak forests in the east, and pines, spruces, and giant redwoods in the west. Some remarkable trees have adapted in ways specific to their local environment. Many western conifers, growing in arid areas prone to summer fires, are able to regenerate after exposure to flame. Others have developed ways of conserving water in desert habitats or have adapted to wet, swampy areas. Today, only fragments of these forests remain, and individual species have become endangered because of overexploitation and habitat loss.

Many species are today cultivated as well as being found in the wild; many others have been introduced and become naturalized. Both of these trends have an impact on wild populations. For trees cultivated since precolonial times, it is often difficult to ascertain the original native ranges since they were often moved around by people as they migrated across the plains cultivating useful plants. In other cases, introduced species may outcompete local, endemic species and thereby artificially change the makeup of local habitats. Nevertheless, fine examples of native American forest remain, many in the national parks.

WHAT IS A TREE?

Trees are woody plants which have a single, well-developed main stem or trunk which branches well above ground level, usually at a height of 6ft or more. The trunk and main branches are covered with a protective layer of bark. These are the only features which all trees have in common as trees do not belong to a single group of plants but are found in many different and unrelated plant families.

The division between shrubs and trees is rather blurred. Shrubs are also woody plants but are generally smaller, with several stems which branch at or near ground level. All of the species in this book will form trees where conditions are appropriate.

Unlike non-woody plants, trees grow in both height and girth each year. The increase in height is achieved simply by the elongation of the branches. The increase in girth is achieved by the addition of an extra layer of woody tissue on the trunk and branches. These layers can be seen as the annual rings exposed when a tree is felled.

Trees are often divided into evergreen and deciduous species. **Evergreens** shed and replace their leaves gradually over a period of years. The leaves are often leathery or waxy to reduce water loss or withstand the cold, so evergreens are typical of cold or mountainous regions, but are also common in hot, dry habitats. **Deciduous** trees shed all of their leaves each year, and remain bare through the winter. This allows the trees to remain dormant, husbanding their resources during the harshest season. Their leaves are generally thinner and more delicate than those of evergreens, and are more prone to wilting and frost damage.

Many trees reproduce by means of **flowers**, and the fruits and seeds which develop later. Those species which are wind pollinated often have tiny flowers, lacking sepals and petals; and the flowers appear well before the leaves in spring. Insect-pollinated trees have larger, more showy flowers, which are often produced later in the year. One large group of trees which does not have flowers is the conifers, so-called because of their cone-shaped reproductive organs.

GLOSSARY

Alternate With leaves scattered along the twig.
Anther Fertile tip of a stamen, containing pollen.
Bract Leaflike structure at base of leaf or cone scale.
Capsule Dry fruit usually splitting when ripe to release seeds.
Catkin Slender spike of tiny flowers usually lacking sepals and petals, and wind pollinated.
Cultivar Plant bred by gardeners, not occurring naturally in the wild.
Involucre Leaflike structure, usually green or greenish, surrounding flowers and fruits.
Leaflet Separate division of a leaf.
Native Originating from an area.
Naturalized Fully established in the wild in areas outside original distribution.
Opposite With leaves arranged in pairs along the twig.
Ovary Female part of a flower containing egg cells and, eventually, seeds.
Pinnate Divided into two rows of leaflets along a central axis.
Palmate Divided into leaves which spread from a single point like fingers of a hand.
Semi-evergreen Retaining most leaves in all except the harshest conditions.
Stamen Male part of a flower consisting of a slender stalk bearing the pollen sacks or anthers.
Stipule Small, leaflike structure at the base of the leaf-stalk.
Style Usually a slender organ on top of the ovary bearing a surface receptive to pollen.
Sucker New shoot growing from the roots of a tree.
Twice pinnate With each of the pinnate divisions themselves pinnately divided.
Trifoliolate With three leaflets.

IDENTIFYING TREES

All plants have specific characteristics, or combinations of characteristics, which enable them to be identified, even among species that have a similar overall appearance. Not all features are equally useful or even constant. Plants on rich soils, for example, tend to produce lush growth and may have larger leaves than plants of the same species growing on poor soils. Identifying trees can be more difficult than identifying herbaceous plants simply because the necessary parts are often out of reach and cannot be observed easily. However, with practice, identification can become quite easy. Always examine the tree and its parts closely and be sure you are comparing similar structures and not, for example, mistaking a stipule for a leaflet. The different parts of a tree and the characters they provide are described here as an initial guide to recognition.

The **height** of a tree varies considerably with age, soil depth, exposure, and other environmental factors. The heights given in this book are the maximum normally attained by each species; many individual trees will be smaller. The **crown** of the tree is made up of the branches and twigs. The outline or overall shape is often distinctive although it can vary with age. There may be a recognizable **pattern of branching** and the branches themselves may be arched or pendulous. Conifers often have branches in regular whorls which may clothe the trunk almost to the ground. Most non-coniferous trees have rather irregular branching patterns. **Twigs** can be hairy or colored. These characters generally occur only on young growth as hairs are lost with age, and older twigs become duller and darker. The presence or absence of spines on the twigs is also a useful distinguishing feature. The **trunk** provides few useful characters other than general features such as being short, stout or bare for most of its length.

Bark is less useful than is often supposed for identifying trees, but the overall color, texture, and whether the bark sheds in strips or flakes provide some clues. The texture varies with age to some extent, usually becoming rougher and often more cracked and fissured in old trees. Sometimes the outer layers of bark peel or flake to reveal brighter layers beneath.

Leaves are a major source of identification characters. Start by looking at their arrangement on the twigs: for example, are they alternate (scattered along the twig) or opposite? Are the leaves pinnately (with two rows of leaflets arranged along the central axis) or palmately divided (with leaflets spreading like fingers of a hand)? Are the leaves or leaflets lobed, toothed, or entire? All of these features are relatively constant and reliable. The size of the leaves is also important but spans a range rather than being a precise measurement as it can vary somewhat with age and growing conditions. Other useful features may include texture (whether thin or leathery), color (often different when unfolding in spring and frequently so in autumn), degree of hairiness, and the distribution of hairs on the leaf. Leaves are generally paler and more hairy on the underside than on their upper surface. **Stipules** are small, leaflike organs which occur at the base of the leaf-stalk in some species.

Flowers and **fruits** are also important. Look at the size and shape of the flowers. Are petals present and if so, how many are there and are they of equal size? The way in which the flowers are arranged is often a useful character, for example in spikes or clusters, or scattered singly along the twigs? Also note whether the flowers are borne on new wood, that is the current year's growth, or on old wood which is the lower, thicker parts of the twigs. Many trees have single-sexed flowers: male flowers have only stamens while female ones have an ovary and style but no stamens.

The type of fruit (fleshy, berry-like, dry), together with its size and color when ripe, also provides clues to identity. Only trees with hermaphrodite or female flowers bear fruit.

One group of trees, the **conifers**, bears cones instead of flowers and fruits. It includes firs, pines, and spruces. The pollen-bearing male cones are usually small and sometimes brightly colored. Female cones are larger, and the scales which make up the cone become woody as the seeds ripen. The shape and arrangement of the cone scales are important characteristics.

WHAT NEXT?

There are many opportunities to pursue your interest in native trees. Many organizations are dedicated to raising awareness of them, both at the national level and, especially, regionally. In addition, many arboretums and botanic gardens work for the conservation of native trees and other plants as listed below:

Alaska Botanical Garden (Anchorage, Alaska)
Arnold Arboretum (Jamaica Plain, Massachussets)
Chicago Botanical Garden (Glencoe, Illinois)
Marie Selby Botanical Garden (Sarasota, Florida)
Missouri Botanical Garden (St. Louis, Missouri)
New York Botanic Garden (New York, New York)
Rancho Santa Ana Botanic Garden (Claremont, California)

A wide variety of reference and popular books is dedicated to the trees of North America, or, trees in general:

The Encyclopedia of North American trees, by Sam Benvie. Richmond Hill, Ontario: Firefly Books, 2002.
The Firefly Encyclopedia of Trees, by Steve Cafferty (ed.). Richmond Hill, Ontario: Firefly Books, 2005.
Field Guide to North American Trees (2nd edition), by Thomas Elias. New York: Grolier, 1989.
The National Audubon Society Field Guide to North American Trees: Western Region, by Elbert Luther Little. New York: Knopf, 1980.
Flora of North America, by the Flora of North America Editorial Committee (eds.). New York: Oxford University Press, 2003.

Web Sites
Useful and informative Web sites include the following:

http://www.borealforest.org/index.php. Faculty of Forest and the Environment, Lakehead University, Canada
http://hua.huh.harvard.edu/FNA/. Flora of North America, United States
http://mobot.mobot.org/W3T/Search/vast.html. TROPICOS nomenclatural database, Missouri Botanical Garden
http://www.fs.fed.us/database/feis/index.html. USDA Forest Service

GINKGO FAMILY, GINKGOACEAE

Maidenhair Tree (Ginkgo)
Ginkgo biloba

Deciduous
Up to 100ft

ID FACT FILE

Crown
Conical, irregular

Bark
Gray, becoming
furrowed

Twigs
Greenish-brown,
stout, spurred

Leaves
Scattered or
in clusters,
5×4in, fan-
shaped, usually
deeply 2-lobed,
leathery

Flowers
Males, yellowish
in erect catkins,
females paired,
on separate
trees

Fruits
1¼in, oval,
green ripening
yellow, fleshy,
foul-smelling

Ginkgo is the sole survivor of an ancient lineage of trees, other species only being known from fossils. Most closely related to conifers but in its own distinct family, it is native to China, although now possibly extinct in the wild. It is widely grown in eastern and western states as a large specimen tree with attractive fanlike foliage. The unpleasant-smelling fruits are eaten in China.

PINE FAMILY, PINACEAE

Evergreen
Up to 230ft

J	F	M	A	M	J
J	A	S	O	N	D

Pacific Silver Fir
Abies amabilis

ID FACT FILE

CROWN
Pyramidal

BARK
Smooth and
silvery at first,
becoming
reddish-brown
and scaly

LEAVES
Flattened
needles, ¾–1½in,
grooved and
shiny green
above, silvery
below; spreading
forward in 2 rows
curved forward
along the upper
twigs

CONES
3–6in,
cylindrical, erect,
and purplish on
upper twigs,
cone scales
finely hairy

Native to the coniferous forests of the Pacific
Northwest from Alaska to Oregon where it
favors the cool wet climate, this large attractive
tree with a tapering crown is used for timber
and grown ornamentally. The silvery needles,
which are densely crowded along the twigs,
emit a strong smell of oranges when crushed
or bruised.

PINE FAMILY, PINACEAE

Evergreen
Up to 130ft

Bristlecone Fir
Abies bracteata

This rare, slow-growing fir is native only in the
mountains of southern California, where it is
found in mixed evergreen forests on steep
rocky slopes. It has a narrow conical habit
when young with a finely tapering crown when
mature. The needles have strong silver bands
underneath, contrasting with the shiny green
upper surface. The common name refers to
the distinctive cones, which bear long,
persisting fine, hair-like bracts.

ID FACT FILE

CROWN
Finely tapering
with slightly
drooping
branches, curved
upward at the
tips

BARK
Dark reddish-
brown, smooth at
first, becoming
fissured and
bearing the scars
of fallen
branches

LEAVES
Flattened stiff
needles sharply
pointed,
1½–2¼in, shiny
green above,
silver-banded
below, spreading
in 2 rows

CONES
2½–4in, green or
purplish-brown,
erect on the
upper branches,
each cone scale
bearing a bristle-
like bract

PINE FAMILY, PINACEAE

Evergreen
Up to 165ft

| J | F | M | A | M | J |
| J | A | S | O | N | D |

White Fir
Abies concolor

ID FACT FILE

CROWN
Narrowly
pyramidal

BARK
Gray, smooth at
first becoming
deeply fissured

LEAVES
Flattened almost
stalkless
needles,
1½–2¼in, blue-
green with white
bands on both
surfaces, in 2
rows curving
upward at right
angles to each
other

CONES
3–5in, green
ripening purplish-
brown, erect on
upper branches,
cone scales
finely hairy

This large fir is widespread throughout the
mountainous regions of the west. Retaining a
pyramidal form well into maturity and bearing
attractive blue-green foliage, it is an important
tree for local wildlife. There are two varieties:
var. *concolor* is found in the warm dry Rocky
Mountains; var. *lowiana* is found on the cooler,
wetter, Pacific Coast. It is often planted
outside of its native range for ornament.

PINE FAMILY, PINACEAE

Evergreen
Up to 330ft

J	F	M	A	M	J
J	A	S	O	N	D

Grand Fir
Abies grandis

The Grand Fir is commonly found throughout the Pacific coastal region from southern British Columbia to California, and also in parts of the Rockies. It is a fast-growing tree with distinctive needles arranged comblike along the twigs. Extensively harvested, in modern times for timber, it was formerly used for the medicinal properties of the leaves and bark. Balsam, a resin exuded from blisters found on the bark, has also been used for its sealant properties.

ID FACT FILE

CROWN
Open, narrowly pointed

BARK
Brown, smooth at first with resin blisters, becoming scaly and deeply furrowed

LEAVES
Flattened needles, ¾–1½in, shiny dark green above with 2 silvery bands underneath, spreading in 2 distinct rows at right angles either side of the twigs, aromatic when crushed

CONES
2–4in, cylindrical, erect on upper twigs, green/brown, cone scales hairy

PINE FAMILY, PINACEAE

Evergreen
Up to 100ft

| J | F | M | A | M | J |
| J | A | S | O | N | D |

Alpine Fir
Abies lassiocarpa

Alpine Fir is found at high altitudes, up to the timber line from Alaska and the Yukon in the north, as far south as Arizona, where a southern variety (var. *arizonica*), with bluer leaves and a more corky bark, is found. Important to local wildlife, these trees often form attractive stands of spirelike trees, or may be found growing with spruce and other coniferous or broadleaf trees.

ID FACT FILE

CROWN
Narrowly conical

BARK
Gray, smooth at first with resin blisters, becoming fissured

LEAVES
Flattened needles, ¾–1½in, dark green with white bands on both surfaces, crowded and spreading forward in 2 rows, curving upward on uppermost twigs, aromatic

CONES
2½–4in, cylindrical, erect on upper twigs, purple ripening brown, cone scales finely hairy

PINE FAMILY, PINACEAE

Evergreen
Up to 130ft

| J | F | M | A | M | J |
| J | A | S | O | N | D |

Californian Red Fir
Abies magnifica

ID FACT FILE

CROWN
Conical, open

BARK
Reddish-brown,
thickly furrowed

TWIGS
Stout, brown,
hairy when young

LEAVES
Needle-like,
¾–1in, 4-sided,
curved, blue-
green above with
whitish bands,
spreading in 2
rows

CONES
6–8in,
cylindrical, erect
and purplish on
upper twigs,
cone scales with
fine hairs

A large handsome tree with an attractive form, Californian Red Fir is found in the high ranges of the Cascade Mountains in Oregon and the Coastal Ranges of California. It is also found through the Sierra Nevada Mountains into western Nevada and often forms pure, dense stands. An important habitat tree for a wide range of wildlife and also used for lumber, this species is also widely grown outside of its natural range.

PINE FAMILY, PINACEAE

Evergreen
Up to 230ft

| J | F | M | A | M | J |
| J | A | S | O | N | D |

Noble Fir
Abies procera

ID FACT FILE

CROWN
Conical, rounded
at tip

BARK
Gray, becoming
brown, smooth
with resin
blisters
becoming
fissured when
mature

LEAVES
Flattened
needles, ⅟₁₆–⅛in,
grooved above,
bluish-green with
paler bands and
curved upward

CONES
5–8in,
cylindrical, erect
on upper twigs,
green maturing
brown, cone
scales covered
by large toothed,
papery bracts
pointing
downward

A large conical tree native to the Cascades and
Coastal Ranges of Washington and Oregon,
this species favors wetter, west-facing slopes. It
has large attractive cones covered with papery
bracts. It is often grown ornamentally outside
its range and the timber is also highly prized
for its light weight and high strength. Fallen
trees often act as nursery beds for seedlings,
found growing in lines along decaying trunks.
It is known to hybridize readily with
Californian Red Fir (*Abies magnifica*) and
hybrid swarms intermediate between the two
species can be seen in northern California and
southern Oregon where both species are found
together. As well as being cultivated
ornamentally the wood of this species is used
for light construction on account of its relative
strength compared to other fir species.
Additionally, Noble Fir also forms a high
percentage of trees sold as Christmas trees,
and the foliage is also utilized for floristry.

PINE FAMILY, PINACEAE

Deciduous
Up to 50ft

J	F	M	A	M	J
J	A	S	O	N	D

Subalpine Larch
Larix lyalli

Found from Montana west to central
Washington and in adjacent parts of Canada,
Subalpine Larch is a species of high elevations,
often forming the timber line, and is usually seen
in pure stands between 5,000 and 6,500ft. It is
an attractive and long-lived species, although
rarely seen, owing to its isolated habitat.
Although not often found in cultivation, it is an
important habitat tree in its natural range.

ID FACT FILE

CROWN
Narrow to
irregular and
spreading

BARK
Gray, smooth
becoming
reddish-gray and
fissured into
plates

TWIGS
Densely whitish-
hairy, spurred

LEAVES
Needle-like,
flattened, 1in,
scattered and
alternate on long
shoots, crowded
in clusters on
spur shoots,
pale blue-green
turning yellow in
autumn

CONES
1½–2in, elliptical,
erect, cone
scales hairy, with
long, pointed
bracts, brown

PINE FAMILY, PINACEAE

Deciduous
Up to 200ft

J	F	M	A	M	J
J	A	S	O	N	D

Western Larch
Larix occidentalis

ID FACT FILE

CROWN
Conical

BARK
Reddish-brown,
scaly, becoming
furrowed forming
thin flat plates

TWIGS
Brown, stout,
usually hairless,
spurred

LEAVES
Needle-like,
flattened,
¾–1½in,
scattered and
alternate on long
shoots, crowded
in clusters on
spur shoots, light
green turning
yellow in autumn

CONES
¾–1½in,
elliptical, erect,
cone scales
rounded, hairy,
overlapping, with
long, pointed
bracts, brown

The largest of all the larch species, this tree is
found in the mountains of British Columbia,
south to Oregon. Long-lived (to 400 years), it is
an important timber tree and also an important
habitat constituent for many small mammals and
birds. Although occasionally cultivated, it rarely
reaches its full potential outside its native range.

PINE FAMILY, PINACEAE

Evergreen
Up to 100ft

J	F	M	A	M	J
J	A	S	O	N	D

Brewer's Weeping Spruce
Picea breweriana

ID FACT FILE

CROWN
Pyramidal,
shoots and
foliage weeping

BARK
Reddish-brown,
becoming
fissured and
scaly

TWIGS
Reddish-brown,
downy

LEAVES
Needle-like,
flattened,
¾–1½in, fleshy,
blunt, dark green
above, green
below with 2
white bands,
radiating on
shoots, borne on
short pegs

CONES
4–5in, narrowly
oval, purple
ripening brown,
pendulous when
mature, cone
scales rounded

Easily identifiable by its unusual weeping habit, Brewer's Weeping Spruce is a slow-growing tree restricted to the mountains of Oregon and California, where it occurs sporadically in mixed coniferous forests. The distinctive weeping habit is also why the species is highly valued as an ornamental tree although it rarely attains its potential height when in cultivation.

PINE FAMILY, PINACEAE

Evergreen
Up to 165ft

J	F	M	A	M	J
J	A	S	O	N	D

Engelmann's Spruce
Picea engelmannii

Usually found at high elevations often in pure stands, this important timber tree is found largely in the Rocky Mountains. Localized populations can also be found throughout Washington, Oregon, Colorado, and New Mexico. The bluish foliage resembles that of the blue form of the related Colorado or Blue Spruce (*P. pungens*). Many ornamental varieties exist and the foliage of cultivated forms often smells unpleasant when crushed.

ID FACT FILE

CROWN
Conical

BARK
Reddish-brown, becoming gray-brown and fissured into large scales

TWIGS
Brown, slender, hairy

LEAVES
Needle-like, flattened, ⅜–1in, 4-angled, flexible, pointed, dark blue-green with white bands, smelling unpleasant when crushed, borne on short pegs

CONES
1½–3in, cylindrical, brown, pendulous when mature, cone scales long, toothed

Evergreen
Up to 100ft

| J | F | M | A | M | J |
| J | A | S | O | N | D |

White Spruce
Picea glauca

ID FACT FILE

CROWN
Narrowly conical

BARK
Gray to brown,
smooth
becoming scaly

TWIGS
Reddish-brown,
slender, hairless

LEAVES
Needle-like,
flattened, ½–¾in,
4-angled,
stiff, pointed,
spreading on
upper side
of twig, blue-
green with white
bands, smelling
unpleasant when
crushed, borne
on short pegs

CONES
1½–2½in,
cylindrical, brown,
pendulous when
mature, cone
scales rounded

White Spruce is one of the most widely
distributed conifer species across North
America, and is found across the breadth of the
north of the continent from Alaska to the east
of Canada, south into Maine and Minnesota
with isolated populations in Montana, the
Dakotas, and Wyoming. In its native range it is
one of the most important timber trees used
for construction and is also widely used in
reforestation and as a shelterbelt tree. In
common with *P. engelmanni*, the resonant
wood is also used to make musical instruments.

PINE FAMILY, PINACEAE

Evergreen
Up to 60ft

J	F	M	A	M	J
J	A	S	O	N	D

Black Spruce
Picea mariana

ID FACT FILE

CROWN
Narrowly conical, with lower branches drooping

BARK
Dark gray, becoming scaly

TWIGS
Reddish-brown, slender, hairy

LEAVES
Needle-like, flattened, ⅜–⅝in, 4-angled, stiff, pointed, spreading, blue-green with white bands, borne on short pegs

CONES
½–1¼in, egg-shaped, curved brown, pendulous when mature, remaining on tree for many years, cone scales toothed

This species, like White Spruce, is also transcontinental across Canada to Alaska, although only ranging south as far as New Jersey and Minnesota. It is also used for much the same range of uses as the related *P. glauca*, although is more limited as a construction timber due to its smaller size. It grows easily from seed but also propagates itself by layering where the lower branches, weighed down by snow, take root in the ground. Often in bogs known as muskegs.

PINE FAMILY, PINACEAE

Evergreen
Up to 100ft

Colorado or Blue Spruce

Picea pungens

This species is found in the southern Rocky
Mountains of the south-western United States.
It favors dry mountain slopes and has developed
a thick waxy cuticle on its needles in the
southern part of its range to protect it from the
fierce sunlight found there. A distinct variety,
P. pungens var. *glauca*, has strongly blue-green
foliage instead of the normal gray to blue-green,
and it is this form which is most widely grown
as an ornamental.

ID FACT FILE

CROWN
Conical

BARK
Dark brown,
furrowed and
scaly

TWIGS
Brown, stout,
hairless

LEAVES
Needle-like, 1in,
4-angled, stiff,
sharply pointed,
spreading, gray
to blue-green,
borne on short
pegs

CONES
2½–4in,
cylindrical,
brown,
pendulous when
mature, cone
scales long,
narrow,
irregularly
toothed

PINE FAMILY, PINACEAE

Evergreen
Up to 200ft

J	F	M	A	M	J
J	A	S	O	N	D

Sitka Spruce
Picea sitchensis

ID FACT FILE

CROWN
Conical

BARK
Gray, smooth,
becoming scaly
and peeling

TWIGS
Brown, stout,
hairless

LEAVES
Needle-like, 1in,
flattened, stiff,
pointed,
spreading, dark
green with
whitish bands
below, borne on
short pegs

CONES
2½–4in,
cylindrical,
orange-brown,
pendulous when
mature, cone
scales long,
rounded,
irregularly
toothed

Sitka Spruce is a fast-growing tree and the
tallest of the spruces; it may even exceed
the suggested height under good
conditions. It is a native of temperate rain
forests from Alaska south to California and
is named after Sitka Island in Alaska. It can
increase in height by up to 3ft per year
which makes it a popular choice for
commercial forestry. Conversely, its large
size makes it generally unsuitable as an
ornamental tree.

Evergreen
Up to 50ft

| J | F | M | A | M | J |
| J | A | S | O | N | D |

Whitebark Pine
Pinus albicaulis

ID FACT FILE

CROWN
Open, irregular

BARK
Gray, smooth,
becoming
reddish-brown,
fissured and
scaly

TWIGS
Brown, hairy
when young

LEAVES
Needle-like,
1½–3in, pointed,
in clusters of 5
crowded toward
ends of twigs,
yellow-green
flecked white

CONES
2½–3¼in,
globular, brown,
cone scales with
sharp spine, only
opening on decay

Whitebark pine is found in scattered populations at high elevations, above 3,000ft on rocky dry slopes up to the timber line. It ranges from British Columbia and Alberta in Canada in the north, south to the Sierra Nevada Mountains in California and also along the Rockies to Wyoming. Often attaining a rugged appearance due to the windswept, exposed situations in which it occurs, Whitebark Pine is an important habitat tree and the seeds were also formerly harvested by people.

PINE FAMILY, PINACEAE

Evergreen
Up to 50ft

J	F	M	A	M	J
J	A	S	O	N	D

Colorado Pine
Pinus aristata

ID FACT FILE

CROWN
Irregular, spreading

BARK
Gray, smooth, becoming fissured and reddish-brown

TWIGS
Densely clothed with needles

LEAVES
Needle-like, ¾–1½in, stiff, blunt-pointed, in clusters of 5 crowded along stem, dark green flecked white, persistent for many years

CONES
2½–4in, oval, reddish-brown, cone scales with sharp spine

This species is native to the Rocky Mountains of Colorado and New Mexico and is often found in pure stands in exposed, dry sites. Although not often seen planted ornamentally, it is extremely hardy. However, it will generally not reach its potential height in cultivation, making it potentially suitable for garden rockeries. It is very long lived, perhaps to 3,000 years.

PINE FAMILY, PINACEAE

Evergreen
Up to 80ft

J	F	M	A	M	J
J	A	S	O	N	D

Knobcone Pine
Pinus attenuata

ID FACT FILE

CROWN
Conical, or
irregular

BARK
Gray, smooth,
becoming
fissured and
scaly

TWIGS
Brown, hairy
when young

LEAVES
Needle-like,
3–7in, slender,
in clusters of 3,
yellow-green

CONES
4–8in, globular,
brown, in whorls,
cone scales
raised, conical,
with sharp spine

Like most pines, Knobcone Pine has adapted
to survive the forest fires that are common
where it occurs, and the mature cones on this
particular tree can remain dormant for as many
as 30 years, before opening after fire. It is found
inland, from Oregon south through California
to Baja California, on exposed rocky mountain
soils to over 3,000ft in the south of its range,
lower in the north. Cone scales are to an
extent, conical rather than rounded, giving the
mature cones a somewhat knobbly appearance.

PINE FAMILY, PINACEAE

Evergreen
Up to 50ft

| J | F | M | A | M | J |
| J | A | S | O | N | D |

Mexican Pinyon
Pinus cembroides

ID FACT FILE

CROWN
Rounded to
irregular

BARK
Gray, smooth,
becoming
furrowed with
reddish inner
bark

TWIGS
Brown, hairy
when young

LEAVES
Needle-like,
¾–2½in, pointed,
in clusters of 3,
dark green

CONES
1–2in, globular,
reddish-brown,
resinous, cone
scales thick, with
small spine

Largely Mexican in its distribution, this pinyon
extends across the border into the United
States to southern Arizona, New Mexico, and
central Texas, with a closely related species
P. edulis ranging as far north as the southern
Rockies. It is a species of rocky mountain
slopes and is usually found growing with other
pinyons and junipers at elevations up to
6,500ft. It is usually smaller in the wild,
although in cultivation it can reach the given
height. The seeds are edible and consumed
either raw or roasted and are harvested on a
commercial basis, especially in Mexico.

PINE FAMILY, PINACEAE

Evergreen
Up to 100ft

| J | F | M | A | M | J |
| J | A | S | O | N | D |

Lodgepole Pine
Pinus contorta

ID FACT FILE

CROWN
Small and rounded, to tall and conical

BARK
Dark brown and thickly furrowed, or light brown, thin and scaly

TWIGS
Densely clothed with needles

LEAVES
Needle-like, 1¼–3in, slender, paired, twisted, pointed, yellow-green

CONES
¾–2½in, oval, reddish-brown, cone scales with slender spine, sometimes persistent for many years

This is a very variable species with perhaps three distinct subspecies recognized. Shore pine (ssp. *contorta*) is found on the Pacific Coast from Alaska to California and named for the gnarled, twisted branches contorted by prevailing winds. It itself is also often divided into two groups, a northern form and a southern one which some treat as distinct. The inland subspecies (ssp. *latifolia*) is found in the Rocky Mountains and differs from the species in having a tall slender trunk and thin scaly bark. It was previously used to support lodges, hence the name Lodgepole Pine. A third subspecies (ssp. *murrayana*) is also sometimes recognized from the Cascade and Sierra Nevada Mountains, but this differs only slightly from the Lodgepole Pine. Although previously much used for its antiseptic properties it is no longer used for medicinal purposes. As with many other pine species, various parts of the tree have formerly been exploited, including the leaves as a source of a dye, and resins as a source of pitch. However, neither these nor other properties are exploited commercially today.

PINE FAMILY, PINACEAE

Evergreen
Up to 35ft

ID FACT FILE

CROWN
Rounded to
irregular

BARK
Gray, smooth,
becoming
furrowed with
reddish inner
bark

TWIGS
Brown, hairy
when young

LEAVES
Needle-like,
¾–1½in, pointed,
in clusters of 2,
dark green

CONES
1½–2in, globular,
yellow-brown,
resinous, cone
scales thick, with
small spine

Pinyon
Pinus edulis

Previously considered as a northern variety of
Mexican Pinyon (*P. cembroides*), this tree is
now considered as a distinct species. It is found
in the southern Rockies south to Mexico with
localized scattered populations in Oklahoma and
California. This species is commonly used for
the edible seeds in the United States, and the
wood which is aromatic, is used as a fuel wood.

PINE FAMILY, PINACEAE

Evergreen
Up to 70ft

J	F	M	A	M	J
J	A	S	O	N	D

Apache Pine
Pinus engelmanii

ID FACT FILE

CROWN
Open, columnar

BARK
Dark brown,
rough and
fissured into
plates

TWIGS
Brown, hairy
when young

LEAVES
Needle-like,
8–16in, stiff, in
clusters of 3 or
sometimes 5,
drooping, green

CONES
4–6½in, oval,
brown, shiny,
cone scales
thick, with small
spine

Previously considered a variety of the
Pondersosa Pine (*P. ponderosa*), to which it is
closely related, Apache Pine is now treated as a
distinct species. It is generally a Mexican
species found in the Sierra Madre Occidental,
but crosses into the United States, where it
grows on mountain ridges and slopes in New
Mexico and Arizona. The seedlings spend a
few years in a grasslike stage with a short stem
and long needles before renewing upward
growth. It is too rare to be used for its wood,
although the inner bark was previously used as
a food stuff.

PINE FAMILY, PINACEAE

Evergreen
Up to 50ft

J	F	M	A	M	J
J	A	S	O	N	D

Limber Pine
Pinus flexilis

ID FACT FILE

CROWN
Conical,
becoming open
and irregular

BARK
Gray, darkening
and becoming
fissured with age

TWIGS
Brown, hairy
when young,
flexible

LEAVES
Needle-like,
½–⅜in, pointed in
clusters of 5
toward the ends
of twigs, green
with whitish lines

CONES
3–6in, oval,
brown, shiny,
cone scales
thick, with small
spine

An important montane pine found throughout
the Rocky Mountains from Canada to Mexico.
Limber Pine is found at high elevations
(6,500–11,200ft). At this height, especially in
the south, it provides a valuable habitat and
food for a variety of animals and birds found at
high altitudes. It is often stunted and gnarled
when found in exposed situations, but will
exceed the given height when grown in
cultivation. The name refers to the pliability
of the young twigs, which can be bent
and knotted.

PINE FAMILY, PINACEAE

Evergreen
Up to 130ft

J	F	M	A	M	J
J	A	S	O	N	D

Jeffrey Pine
Pinus jeffreyi

ID FACT FILE

CROWN
Conical

BARK
Reddish-brown,
furrowed
becoming scaly

TWIGS
Gray, hairless,
scented of
vanilla

LEAVES
Needle-like,
4–10in, slender,
in threes, stiff,
blue-green with
whitish bands

CONES
5–10in, ovoid,
reddish-brown,
cone scales with
slender, recurved
spine

Jeffrey Pine is found in the Sierra Nevada Mountains from Oregon to Nevada and California, and also known from northern Baja California. Sometimes·considered as a variety of the Ponderosa Pine (*P. ponderosa*), this is a species of high elevations, most commonly found above 6,000ft. It is a large stately tree with attractive habit and blue-green foliage and vanilla-scented shoots.

PINE FAMILY, PINACEAE

Evergreen
Up to 200ft

ID FACT FILE

CROWN
Conical

BARK
Gray, darkening
and becoming
fissured with age

TWIGS
Brown, hairy
when young

LEAVES
Needle-like,
3–4in, twisted,
pointed, in
clusters of 5,
blue-green with
whitish lines

CONES
Up to 20in,
cylindrical,
brown, shiny,
cone scales
thick, rounded,
blunt

Sugar Pine
Pinus lambertiana

A giant tree, second only to the redwoods in
terms of mass, Sugar Pine also has the largest
cones of all pine species. It is found in the
Coastal Ranges from Oregon to California and
the Sierra Nevada Mountains at elevations over
10,000ft in the south of its range, lower in the
north. It is so called for the sweetish resin the
bark produces when wounded, formerly used
as a gum. It was an especially important
lumber tree in the early days of settlement of
the West, used for a variety of purposes.
Although fast growing and reputedly relatively
long-lived, perhaps to 800 years, logging of this
species, which continues today in common
with other sought after lumber trees, exceeds
the rate of new growth.

PINE FAMILY, PINACEAE

Evergreen
Up to 50ft

J	F	M	A	M	J
J	A	S	O	N	D

ID FACT FILE

CROWN
Irregular,
spreading

BARK
Gray, smooth,
becoming
fissured and
reddish-brown

TWIGS
Densely clothed
with needles

LEAVES
Needle-like,
¾–1½in, stiff,
blunt-pointed, in
clusters of 5
crowded along
stem, gray-green,
slightly flecked
white, persistent
for many years

CONES
2½–4in, oval,
reddish-brown,
cone scales with
sharp spine

Intermountain Bristlecone Pine

Pinus longaeva

Sometimes considered as a distinct species,
this western variety of *Pinus aristata*—found in
Nevada and Utah, and west to California—
includes the oldest known trees, over 4,500
years old. It may even live as long as 5,000
years. It naturally occurs in extremely
inhospitable exposed mountain habitats where
with age, it becomes gnarled and twisted. As
well as being geographically distinct from the
species, it also differs in having slightly
different colored, and finer foliage.

PINE FAMILY, PINACEAE

Evergreen
Up to 30ft

Singleleaf Pinyon
Pinus monophylla

ID FACT FILE

CROWN
Rounded to
irregular

BARK
Gray-brown,
becoming
furrowed and
scaly

TWIGS
Brown, hairy
when young

LEAVES
Needle-like,
1–2in, pointed,
occurring singly,
gray-green with
whitish lines

CONES
1½–3in, globular,
reddish-brown,
shiny, cone
scales raised,
with small spine

Singleleaf Pinyon is easily recognized by the
unique single needles rather than bundles as is
usual in other pine species. It ranges from
southern Idaho through Utah, Nevada,
California, and Arizona and is usually found
growing with other pinyons or junipers on
rocky mountain slopes or in pure stands in
open groves. The seeds are edible and were
formerly an important food source, and the
wood was also used as a fuel wood and for
fencing.

Evergreen
Up to 200ft

| J | F | M | A | M | J |
| J | A | S | O | N | D |

PINE FAMILY, PINACEAE

Western White Pine
Pinus monticola

ID FACT FILE

CROWN
Narrowly conical
to rounded

BARK
Gray, becoming
furrowed and
scaly

TWIGS
Brown, hairy

LEAVES
Needle-like,
2–4in, in clusters
of 5, blue-green
with whitish lines

CONES
Up to 12in,
cylindrical,
brown, shiny,
cone scales
rounded, with
small spine

A large and important timber tree, Western White Pine ranges from British Columbia in Canada south through the Rockies to Montana, and also along the Coastal Ranges and Sierra Nevada to central California. Formerly widely used for timber, it now suffers badly from white pine blister rust, which ravages this and other similar pine species, although resistant strains are being developed. Trees exceeding 100ft today are rare. The bark and resin were also formerly used, for medicinal properties.

PINE FAMILY, PINACEAE

Evergreen
Up to 80ft

J	F	M	A	M	J
J	A	S	O	N	D

Bishop Pine
Pinus muricata

ID FACT FILE

CROWN
Narrowly conical
to rounded

BARK
Gray-brown,
thick, furrowed
and scaly

TWIGS
Orange, hairy
when young

LEAVES
Needle-like,
4–6in, flattened,
in dense clusters
of 2, green

CONES
2–4in, conical,
brown, shiny, in
clusters, cone
scales raised,
with curved
spine

Bishop Pine is now very rare in the wild, and is only found on the coast of California and on Santa Cruz and Santa Rosa islands offshore. It is remarkable for its cones, which may persist for many, many years and even be overgrown by the bark, and which do not open until the occurrence of fire. It is used to an extent in reforestation and also occasionally seen in cultivation where it is grown as an alternative to the Monterey Pine (*P. radiata*), to which it is somewhat similar.

PINE FAMILY, PINACEAE

Evergreen
Up to 165ft

J	F	M	A	M	J
J	A	S	O	N	D

Ponderosa Pine
Pinus ponderosa

ID FACT FILE

CROWN
Conical,
becoming
irregular

BARK
Dark brown and
ridged when
young, becoming
yellow-brown,
furrowed and
scaly

TWIGS
Densely clothed
with needles

LEAVES
Needle-like,
4–10in, slender,
paired or in 3s or
5s, stiff, curved,
yellowish-green
with whitish
bands

CONES
3–6in, egg-
shaped, shiny
reddish-brown, in
clusters, cone
scales ridged
with an erect
spine

Forming a large conical tree, this is the most
common species of pine in North America. It
also has the widest distribution, south from
British Columbia throughout the western
states as far south as Mexico and as far east as
the Dakotas, ranging from sea level to over
6,000ft. Three distinct subspecies are
recognized: var. *ponderosa*, with needles in
threes found along the coast; var. *scopulorum*,
with needles paired found in the Rocky
Mountains; and var. *arizonica*, with needles in
fives. The wood is used in fine carpentry work.

PINE FAMILY, PINACEAE

Evergreen
Up to 33ft

J	F	M	A	M	J
J	A	S	O	N	D

Parry Pinyon
Pinus quadrifolia

ID FACT FILE

CROWN
Rounded

BARK
Gray, becoming
reddish-brown,
fissured and
scaly

TWIGS
Orange-brown,
hairy

LEAVES
Needle-like,
1¼–2½in,
pointed, curved,
usually in
clusters of 4,
sometimes 2 or
5, dark green

CONES
1¼–2in, conical
to rounded,
yellow-brown,
resinous, cone
scales thick, with
small spine

Parry Pinyon has edible nuts and although
these are not harvested commercially, due
to the restricted distribution of the species,
they are widely consumed by native birds
and animals, which also benefit from the
shelter the tree provides. It is known only
from southern California and Baja
California, where it grows on rocky slopes
usually between 3,000ft and 6,000ft.
Sometimes found in pure stands, it is more
likely to be seen growing with other pinyon
species or junipers.

PINE FAMILY, PINACEAE

Evergreen
Up to 130ft

Monterey Pine
Pinus radiata

ID FACT FILE

CROWN
Densely rounded,
becoming open
and irregular in
exposed areas

BARK
Reddish-brown,
deeply ridged
and furrowed

TWIGS
Slender, with
needles
adpressed along
shoots

LEAVES
Needle-like,
4–6in, slender,
in 3s, pointed,
shiny dark green

CONES
3–6in, egg-
shaped, shiny
brown, in
clusters,
recurved when
mature, cone
scales rounded,
persistent for
many years

An extremely rare species in the wild,
Monterey Pine is known only from three
localities on the coast of California, and from
Guadalupe Island off the Mexican coast.
However, it is a very common tree in
cultivation, in the United States and Western
Europe as an ornamental tree, and also widely
in the Southern Hemisphere (where pines are
not native) as a commercial forestry species.
Fast growing, it only releases its seeds when
exposed to high temperatures, an adaptation to
its native habitat where forest fires are
common.

PINE FAMILY, PINACEAE

Evergreen
Up to 65ft

| J | F | M | A | M | J |
| J | A | S | O | N | D |

Digger Pine
Pinus sabiniana

ID FACT FILE

CROWN
Densely rounded, becoming open and irregular

BARK
Dark gray, thick, becoming fissured, ridged and scaly

TWIGS
Reddish-brown, slender

LEAVES
Needle-like, 8–12in, slender, in 3s, blue-green with whitish lines

CONES
6–10in, egg-shaped, brown, cone scales thick, with curved spine, persistent for many years

This common pine, widespread throughout the Coastal Ranges of California and the Sierra Nevada Mountains, is usually found as scattered individuals although sometimes also in pure stands. It is a fairly adaptable species thriving in a variety of soil conditions and this, together with its attractive glaucous foliage, make it suitable for growing as an ornamental specimen. In the past, seeds and roots were harvested for food, but the timber is of little use except as a fuel wood.

PINE FAMILY, PINACEAE

Evergreen
Up to 100ft

J	F	M	A	M	J
J	A	S	O	N	D

Southwestern White Pine
Pinus strobiformis

ID FACT FILE

CROWN
Columnar, open

BARK
Gray-brown,
deeply furrowed
and ridged

TWIGS
Reddish-brown,
hairy when young

LEAVES
Needle-like,
2½–5in, slender,
usually in
clusters of 5,
blue-green

CONES
Up to 12in,
cylindrical, dark
brown, cone
scales thick, with
small spine

Although it is a large attractive tree,
Southwestern White Pine is not often seen in
cultivation. It has a very restricted range, only
occurring in the United States along the
Mexican border in Texas, Arizona, and New
Mexico in canyons and mountains at high
elevations up to 10,000ft. It is closely related to
Limber Pine (*P. flexilis*), a more widespread
northern species which it also resembles. The
two species, however, do not overlap in their
range and although once considered as
separate varieties of the same species, are now
considered distinct.

PINE FAMILY, PINACEAE

Evergreen
Up to 120ft

J	F	M	A	M	J
J	A	S	O	N	D

ID FACT FILE

CROWN
Rounded and
spreading,
becoming
irregular and
flat-topped

BARK
Reddish-brown
and scaly lower
down, paler and
papery higher up

TWIGS
Reddish-brown,
slender

LEAVES
Needle-like,
1–3in, slender,
in pairs, twisted,
blue-green

CONES
1–3in, egg-
shaped, in
clusters, reddish-
brown, ripening
gray in second
year, cone
scales flat, with
a small spine

Scots Pine
Pinus sylvestris

This species is native across Europe, although
now much reduced in range, and introduced
across the United States as a shelterbelt and
ornamental tree, where it has become
naturalized in many areas in the northeast. Scots
Pine is a useful timber tree and is important for
wildlife in its native habitat; in the United States,
native species better fulfill these purposes
although young trees are often used as
Christmas trees.

PINE FAMILY, PINACEAE

Torrey Pine
Pinus torreyana

ID FACT FILE

CROWN
Conical,
becoming open
and spreading

BARK
Dark brown,
furrowed and
scaly

TWIGS
Green, becoming
gray

LEAVES
Needle-like,
8–13in, usually
in clusters of 5
at ends of twigs,
blue-green

CONES
Up to 6in, oval,
brown, cone
scales thick, with
sharp spine

Evergreen
Up to 50ft

Torrey Pine is a slow-growing tree in the wild,
endemic to California and the rarest of the
North American pines. It is found as isolated
individuals in exposed situations where it often
has a contorted appearance. Current
populations, on Santa Rosa Island and on the
nearby mainland of San Diego County, are
thought to be relicts of a previously much
wider distribution. It is, though, also grown in
cultivation as an ornamental, and outside the
United States as a potential timber tree.

PINE FAMILY, PINACEAE

Evergreen
Up to 100ft

J	F	M	A	M	J
J	A	S	O	N	D

Bigcone Douglas Fir
Pseudotsuga macrocarpa

ID FACT FILE

CROWN
Pyramidal

BARK
Reddish-brown, thick, ridged, corky

TWIGS
Brown, drooping, hairy when young

LEAVES
Needle-like, 1½in, spreading in 2 rows, blue-green, with 2 white bands below, aromatic when bruised

CONES
4–7in, egg-shaped, brown, pendulous, cone scales rounded, with a 3-toothed, barely projecting bract

Bigcone Douglas Fir has a much more restricted range than the related Douglas Fir (*P. menziesii*), and is endemic to southern California, where it is usually found on dry, steep slopes up to an elevation of nearly 10,000ft. It can be easily distinguished from its relative by its large cones and more blue-green foliage. It is adapted to fire and an important habitat tree, but its wood is generally not used due to the restricted distribution of the species.

PINE FAMILY, PINACEAE

Evergreen
Up to 330ft

| J | F | M | A | M | J |
| J | A | S | O | N | D |

Douglas Fir
Pseudotsuga menziesii

ID FACT FILE

CROWN
Pyramidal, with distinctive irregular whorls of branches

BARK
Gray to reddish-brown, ridged, corky

TWIGS
Brown, slender, with pointed, slender, reddish-brown buds

LEAVES
Needle-like, ¾–1½in, spreading in 2 rows, dark green, with 2 white bands below, aromatic when bruised

CONES
2–4in, egg-shaped, brown, pendulous, cone scales rounded, with a 3-toothed, projecting bract

Although potentially reaching a height of more than 330ft, living specimens today rarely exceed 270ft. There are 2 distinct varieties: var. *menziesii*, found along the Pacific Coast from Canada south to central California; and var. *glauca*, which occurs in the Rocky Mountains south to Mexico. Douglas Fir is the most important timber tree in the United States, especially the coastal variety, which also attains the greater height. The bark has medicinal properties and the young trees are also widely used as Christmas trees.

PINE FAMILY, PINACEAE

Evergreen
Up to 200ft

J	F	M	A	M	J
J	A	S	O	N	D

Western Hemlock
Tsuga heterophylla

The largest of the hemlocks, Western Hemlock is found in two disjunct ranges: along the Pacific Coast from Alaska to California, and also on the western slopes of the Rocky Mountains from Idaho north to British Columbia, where it tends to grow at higher elevations, up to 4,000ft. It is a common tree, found in evergreen forests and thrives in areas subjected to mists and fogs. It is an important timber tree, for paper, pulp, and lumber. It is also the source of a cellulose fiber extensively used in the manufacture of rayon and cellophane amongst other materials.

ID FACT FILE

CROWN
Narrowly conical

BARK
Reddish-brown, thin and scaly, becoming furrowed and ridged

TWIGS
Pale brown, finely hairy, with peglike base

LEAVES
Needle-like, ½–¾in, in 2 rows, flattened, blunt, shiny-green above, paler with 2 whitish bands below, aromatic

CONES
Up to 1in, elliptical, brown, drooping, cone scales spreading

PINE FAMILY, PINACEAE

Evergreen
Up to 100ft

Mountain Hemlock
Tsuga mertensia

ID FACT FILE

CROWN
Narrowly conical

BARK
Gray-brown, thick, deeply furrowed and ridged

TWIGS
Reddish-brown, finely hairy, with peglike base

LEAVES
Needle-like, ½–¾in, spreading radially, flattened, blunt, shiny green above, paler with 2 whitish bands below, aromatic

CONES
Up to 3in, cylindrical, brown, drooping, cone scales spreading

Mountain Hemlock has a similar range to the related Western Hemlock (*T. heterophylla*), although it is not quite as widespread and tends to grow at higher elevations, especially in the south of its range, where it may occur at over 10,000ft. The timber is generally not used due to its remote locality, but being a high-alpine species, it is a valued habitat tree for wildlife, and also important for watershed management.

CYPRESS FAMILY, CUPRESSACEAE

Evergreen
Up to 130ft

J	F	M	A	M	J
J	A	S	O	N	D

Incense Cedar
Calocedrus decurrens

ID FACT FILE

CROWN
Narrowly rounded

BARK
Dark brown,
fissured into
large plates

LEAVES
Scale-like, ⅛–½in,
in whorls of 4
overlapping,
hiding shoots

CONES
¾–1½in, brown,
oblong, with 2
large fertile
scales

A long-lived tree (up to 500 years), Incense Cedar is native to California and Oregon, where it is most common in the Sierra Nevada. It can be found in dry, shady sites with other conifer and oak species up to altitudes of 6,500ft. It has a columnar habit and is sometimes grown ornamentally; the crushed foliage smells of turpentine and the timber is also used due to its durable non-decaying properties. The major source of pencil wood in the US.

CYPRESS FAMILY, CUPRESSACEAE

Evergreen
Up to 200ft

| J | F | M | A | M | J |
| J | A | S | O | N | D |

Lawson Cypress
Chamaecyparis lawsoniana

ID FACT FILE

CROWN
Spirelike, apical
shoots drooping

BARK
Gray-brown,
fibrous, cracked
and furrowed into
large plates

TWIGS
Slender,
flattened,
spreading
horizontally

LEAVES
Scale-like, in
opposite pairs,
1/16–1/8in, pressed
tightly to the
shoot, scented
of parsley, green
above, whitish
below

CONES
3/8in, globular,
reddish-brown, in
clusters, scales
8, blunt

Adapted to the Pacific coastal fog belt, this
species is restricted to California and Oregon
where it forms mixed stands with other
coniferous trees. The timber of this long-lived
tree was previously much used in a variety of
ways; today it is mostly exported to Japan. It is
also much grown as an ornamental and there
are a wide range of forms, from columnar to
weeping, and also many different foliage types.

CYPRESS FAMILY, CUPRESSACEAE

Evergreen
Up to 100ft

J	F	M	A	M	J
J	A	S	O	N	D

ID FACT FILE

CROWN
Conical, apical
shoots drooping

BARK
Gray-brown, thin
becoming fibrous

TWIGS
Flattened,
spreading
horizontally

LEAVES
Scale-like, in
opposite pairs,
⅛in, tips
spreading,
scented of
turpentine, blue-
green

CONES
⅜–½in, globular,
blue ripening
reddish-brown,
scales 8, with
coarse spike in
center

Alaska Cedar
Chamaecyparis nootkatensis

Alaska Cedar is found on the Pacific Coast
from Oregon in the south (where it is usually
found at high elevations), to Alaska in the
north at a range of altitudes, from sea level to
just below the snow line. Long-lived (to 2,000
years or more), it has a long association of use
by humans, especially for marine use. Despite
all parts having an unpleasant, turpentine-like
odor, it is also widely grown ornamentally and
a pendulous form is particularly attractive.

CYPRESS FAMILY, CUPRESSACEAE

Evergreen
Up to 72ft

J	F	M	A	M	J
J	A	S	O	N	D

Arizona Cypress
Cupressus arizonica

ID FACT FILE

CROWN
Pyramidal

BARK
Gray to reddish-
brown, scaly
becoming fibrous

TWIGS
Brownish-orange,
stout

LEAVES
Scale-like, in
opposite pairs,
1/16–1/8in,
overlapping,
pressed closely
against shoot,
blue-green

CONES
1in, globose,
brown, scales
6–8, pointed,
maturing in the
second year

Known only from southern Arizona to the
Chisos Mountains (Texas), and Mexico,
Arizona Cypress is locally common where
found. It is a component of riparian habitats
in rocky canyons to over 5,000ft, sometimes
forming pure, blue-green stands.
Occasionally grown for ornament or as
Christmas trees, the species is otherwise not
widely used on account of its restricted
distribution and occurrence.

CYPRESS FAMILY, CUPRESSACEAE

Evergreen
Up to 100ft

J	F	M	A	M	J
J	A	S	O	N	D

Baker Cypress
Cupressus bakeri

ID FACT FILE

CROWN
Conical

BARK
Reddish-brown,
initially smooth,
then peeling

TWIGS
Brownish,
slender, angled

LEAVES
Scale-like, in
opposite pairs,
1⁄16–1⁄8in, pressed
closely against
shoot, blue-green

CONES
1⁄2–3⁄4in, globose,
brown, scales
6–8, pointed,
often maturing
after several
years and fire

This species is relatively slow-growing and
forms a medium-size tree with pendulous
sprays of blue-green foliage. It is the
northernmost of the cypresses and also the
hardiest, found as far north as southern
Oregon, from where it ranges southward to
California growing at high elevations, usually
between 3,000 and 6,000ft. It is never common
and is usually found in small, scattered
populations in harsh terrain.

CYPRESS FAMILY, CUPRESSACEAE

Evergreen
Up to 100ft

| J | F | M | A | M | J |
| J | A | S | O | N | D |

Gowan Cypress
Cupressus goveniana

ID FACT FILE

CROWN
Conical to
spreading

BARK
Gray-brown,
rough, peeling in
fibrous strips

TWIGS
Slender, brown

LEAVES
Scale-like, in
opposite pairs,
1/16–1/8in,
overlapping,
pressed closely
against shoot,
bright green

CONES
3/8in, globose,
brown to gray,
scales 6–10,
pointed,
maturing in the
second year

This rare localized species has three distinct
recognized varieties, all within California. The
typical variety (var. *goveniana*) is restricted to
two groves in Monterey County and is
generally a small evergreen tree no taller than
30ft. A second variety (var. *pygmaea*), is very
variable, growing no taller than 3ft in the
Mendocino pygmy cypress forest, but
exceeding 80ft in parts of Sonoma County. A
third variety (var. *ambramsiana*), sometimes
recognized as a distinct species, is only found
in the Santa Cruz mountains and Pondersosa
pine forest and can grow as tall as 80ft.

CYPRESS FAMILY, CUPRESSACEAE

Evergreen
Up to 100ft

| J | F | M | A | M | J |
| J | A | S | O | N | D |

Tecate Cypress
Cupressus guadalupensis

ID FACT FILE

CROWN
Spreading

BARK
Reddish-brown,
initially smooth
then peeling

TWIGS
Slender, rounded

LEAVES
Scale-like, in
opposite pairs,
⅛–¼in, pressed
closely against
shoot, green

CONES
½–1½in, globose,
brown, scales
6–8, rounded,
pointed,
maturing after
several years
and fire

The scientific name of this tree refers to the
island off Baja California where it is found, as
well as southern California to the Mexican
border. The common name also refers to the
distribution of this species, relating to Mt.
Tecate. It is always found in small, scattered
populations on rocky slopes of the coastal
mountains. As with many other species of
cypress, the cones do not open to release the
seeds until after fire, allowing the new seedlings
a head start in colonizing new ground.

CYPRESS FAMILY, CUPRESSACEAE

Evergreen
Up to 100ft

J	F	M	A	M	J
J	A	S	O	N	D

Monterey Cypress
Cupressus macrocarpa

ID FACT FILE

CROWN
Broad becoming
spreading

BARK
Gray-brown,
rough, furrowed
and fibrous

TWIGS
Stout, irregular

LEAVES
Scale-like, in
opposite pairs,
$\frac{1}{16}$–$\frac{1}{8}$in,
overlapping,
pressed closely
against shoot,
yellowish-green

CONES
1in, globose,
ripening brown,
scales 8–12,
pointed,
maturing in the
second year

Although widely planted both as an ornamental
tree and a windbreak, this species is
exceedingly rare, now restricted to just two
groves in Monterey County, California. Like
other *Cupressus* species, this tree has the
typical radiating foliage characteristic of the
genus as opposed to the flat, spraylike foliage
exhibited by trees of the related genus,
Chamaecyparis. The species makes an ideal
hedging plant in coastal areas due to its
tolerance of salt spray. Several ornamental
cultivars with variegated foliage or weeping
branches are commercially available.

CYPRESS FAMILY, CUPRESSACEAE

Evergreen
Up to 50ft

J	F	M	A	M	J
J	A	S	O	N	D

Sargent Cypress
Cupressus sargentii

ID FACT FILE

CROWN
Conical to broad

BARK
Gray-brown,
becoming thick
and furrowed

TWIGS
Angled, branched

LEAVES
Scale-like, in
opposite pairs,
up to ⅟₁₆–⅛in,
pressed closely
against shoot,
green with
whitish dot

CONES
1in, globose,
brown, scales
6–8, pointed,
maturing after
several years
and fire

Widely distributed in scattered populations
throughout the Coastal Ranges of California,
this tree is often found in pure stands in open,
dry sites up to an elevation of 3,300ft. It has
the potential to exceed the given height but is
usually a relatively low, spreading tree,
especially in exposed areas. In common with
Macnab Cypress (*C. macnabii*), this species
was extensively used as a fuel wood,
particularly in sites on serpentine rock where
the two species were utilized in the extraction
of mercury.

CYPRESS FAMILY, CUPRESSACEAE

Evergreen
Up to 50ft

J	F	M	A	M	J
J	A	S	O	N	D

California Juniper
Juniperus californica

Native to the Coastal Ranges and Sierra Nevada Mountains of California, this often multistemmed species is found growing in isolated populations in Nevada and Arizona, usually on rocky soils in exposed situations. It will survive periods of drought and prefers a climate of hot, dry summers and mild winters. The fruits are eaten by many birds, and were also formerly ground to provide flour for baking.

ID FACT FILE

CROWN
Irregular, open

BARK
Reddish-brown, fissured and shredding

TWIGS
Pale, slender, hairless

LEAVES
Juvenile foliage needle-like, adult foliage scale-like, in whorls of 3's, ¹⁄₁₆–⅛in, yellow-green

CONES
⅜–⅞in, fleshy, berrylike, globular, blue with a bloom ripening brown

CYPRESS FAMILY, CUPRESSACEAE

Evergreen
Up to 20ft

| J | F | M | A | M | J |
| J | A | S | O | N | D |

Common Juniper
Juniperus communis

The Common Juniper is an extremely widespread species found through Eurasia and across North America in an arc containing much of Canada then south through east-central US states (New York to Minnesota) to South Carolina. It also ranges south from west-central Canada along the Rocky Mountains to Wyoming and Arizona. Juniper is a variable species ranging from a small tree as found in the eastern states, to a low-growing shrub as it occurs in the west, often at high elevations. There are many cultivated varieties varying in form and color.

ID FACT FILE

CROWN
Spreading

BARK
Reddish-brown, scaly and shredding

TWIGS
Pale, slender, hairless

LEAVES
Needle-like, prickly, flattened in whorls of 3, ⅜–1¼in, bluish-green with white band above, yellow-green below

CONES
¼–⅜in, fleshy, berrylike, globular, whitish-blue ripening blue-black in second or third year

CYPRESS FAMILY, CUPRESSACEAE

Evergreen
Up to 65ft

| J | F | M | A | M | J |
| J | A | S | O | N | D |

Alligator Juniper
Juniperus deppeana

ID FACT FILE

Crown
Rounded, becoming irregular

Bark
Gray, furrowed into checkered plates

Twigs
Pale, slender, hairless

Leaves
Juvenile foliage needle-like, adult foliage scale-like, paired, pointed, ¹⁄₁₆–¹⁄₈in, blue-green with whitish dot

Cones
⅜–½in, fleshy, berrylike, globular, brown with a bloom, ripening in second year

This species is the largest of the southwestern junipers, and is most common in the dry mountain ranges of Arizona and New Mexico extending as far east as the Trans Pecos region of western Texas. The species is also widely distributed in Mexico, where up to four varieties are reported. It naturally occurs on dry, rocky mountain slopes associated with other pines and juniper species and is easily recognized by its distinctive checkered bark. It is used as a fuel wood and is relatively long lived, up to 500 years.

CYPRESS FAMILY, CUPRESSACEAE

Evergreen
Up to 30ft

| J | F | M | A | M | J |
| J | A | S | O | N | D |

Oneseed Juniper
Juniperus monosperma

ID FACT FILE

CROWN
Irregular,
spreading

BARK
Gray, shredding

TWIGS
Pale, slender,
hairless, densely
crowded with
foliage

LEAVES
Juvenile foliage
needle-like, adult
foliage scale-like,
paired, ⅟₁₆–⅛in,
yellow-green,
sometimes with
whitish dot

CONES
⅛–¼in, fleshy,
berrylike,
globular, blue
with a bloom,
usually 1-seeded

Found in central Colorado, south to New
Mexico and Arizona, and also Texas on dry
rocky soils and slopes, usually between 3,000
and 6,000ft, Oneseed Juniper is a common
species. It is usually a small tree with several
curved limbs arising from near the base
although it may also be shrublike. As with other
junipers, it is able to slow or even stop growth—
especially during dry, harsh periods—and then
resume once more when conditions improve. It
is used as a fuel wood and the bark was also
formerly used to make matting and clothing.

CYPRESS FAMILY, CUPRESSACEAE

Evergreen
Up to 40ft

J	F	M	A	M	J
J	A	S	O	N	D

Western Juniper
Juniperus occidentalis

ID FACT FILE

CROWN
Irregular,
spreading

BARK
Reddish-brown,
shredding

TWIGS
Pale, slender,
hairless

LEAVES
Juvenile foliage
needle-like, adult
foliage scale-like,
in whorls of 3's,
⅟₁₆–⅛in, gray-
green,
sometimes with
whitish dot

CONES
¼–⅜in, fleshy,
berrylike,
globular, dark
blue with a
bloom, ripening
in second year

Native from Washington to the Sierra Nevada
Mountains of California this is a long-lived
species, up to 2,000 years. Two varieties are
known, var. *occidentalis* and var. *australis*. It is
the latter, restricted to California and with
brown rather than reddish-brown bark, that
attains the greatest age. It grows at high
elevations up to 10,000ft on rocky mountain
slopes where it may develop thickened roots,
which may grow around and over any rocky
outcrops present.

CYPRESS FAMILY, CUPRESSACEAE

Evergreen
Up to 40ft

J	F	M	A	M	J
J	A	S	O	N	D

Utah Juniper
Juniperus osteosperma

ID FACT FILE

CROWN
Spreading

BARK
Reddish-brown to gray, furrowed and shredding

TWIGS
Pale, slender, hairless

LEAVES
Juvenile foliage needle-like, adult foliage scale-like, paired, pointed, $\frac{1}{16}$–$\frac{1}{8}$in, yellow-green

CONES
$\frac{1}{4}$–$\frac{5}{8}$in, fleshy, berrylike, globular, blue with a bloom, ripening brown

Utah Juniper is a relatively common species found as far north as Montana, south to California, Arizona, and New Mexico. It usually prefers hot, dry rocky sites such as exposed mountain slopes. It has a long history of human association, the wood being used for fuel and charcoal, and both the bark and fruits were previously widely used for matting, clothing, and food. It is sometimes grown as an ornamental tree and is also the source of various essential oils. Although of little forage value to wild animals, this species is nevertheless an important habitat tree, providing shelter for a wide variety of small and large animals.

CYPRESS FAMILY, CUPRESSACEAE

Evergreen
Up to 50ft

| J | F | M | A | M | J |
| J | A | S | O | N | D |

Rocky Mountain Juniper
Juniperus scopulorum

ID FACT FILE

CROWN
Rounded, becoming open and irregular

BARK
Reddish-brown to gray, furrowed and shredding

TWIGS
Pale, slender, hairless

LEAVES
Juvenile foliage needle-like, adult foliage scale-like, paired, pointed, $\frac{1}{16}$–$\frac{1}{8}$in, gray-green

CONES
Up to $\frac{3}{8}$in, fleshy, berrylike, globular, blue with a bloom, ripening in the second year

One of the more important horticultural species of juniper, *J. scopulorum* has given rise to numerous cultivars of various forms for use as ornamental trees, including prostrate kinds for ground cover. It naturally ranges from British Columbia and Alberta in Canada, south through the Dakotas to Texas, New Mexico, and Arizona. It is found in a wide variety of habitats: from high, open woodland in the north of its range to limestone bluffs in foothills in the south. The wood is aromatic and used for furniture and also fencing, and like Utah Juniper, it is also the source for various essential oils.

CYPRESS FAMILY, CUPRESSACEAE

Evergreen
Up to 300ft

| J | F | M | A | M | J |
| J | A | S | O | N | D |

Giant Sequoia
Sequoiadendron giganteum

ID FACT FILE

CROWN
Narrowly conical,
with enlarged
buttressed base

BARK
Reddish-brown,
thick, fibrous,
soft

TWIGS
Brown, slender,
drooping

LEAVES
Scale-like, ⅛–⅜in,
spreading
radially forward,
overlapping, dark
green with 2
white bands
below

CONES
2–3in, elliptical,
brown, cone
scales pointed,
ripening in
second year

In common with Redwood, this related species is also endemic to the western coast of America, only being found on the western slopes of the Sierra Nevada Mountains in California. It is an important component of the restricted forests where it still occurs naturally, although it is no longer logged commercially. Smaller than the Redwood it is, however, a denser tree and recognized as the species with the greatest mass in the world. It is also relatively long-lived, to more than 3,000 years.

CYPRESS FAMILY, CUPRESSACEAE

Evergreen
Up to 360ft

J	F	M	A	M	J
J	A	S	O	N	D

Redwood
Sequoia sempervirens

Once more widely distributed, Redwood is now restricted to a narrow coastal strip from southern Oregon to central California. Although not especially long-lived compared to some other conifer species, the oldest trees known being no more than 2,000 years old, this species is the world's tallest tree. It is native to coastal hills that experience constant sea mist. It is an important timber tree and even today is selectively logged, although the practice is controversial.

ID FACT FILE

CROWN
Conical, becoming columnar

BARK
Reddish-brown, thick, fibrous, furrowed

TWIGS
Greenish, slender, forking

LEAVES
Scale-like on leading shoots up to ¼in, spreading radially, needle-like elsewhere, ¼–⅜in, flattened, pointed, spreading in 2 rows, dark green with 2 white bands below

CONES
⅝–1¼in, elliptical, brown, cone scales pointed, ripening in second year

Evergreen
Up to 210ft

| J | F | M | A | M | J |
| J | A | S | O | N | D |

Western Red Cedar
Thuja plicata

ID FACT FILE

CROWN
Narrow, conical
with enlarged
buttressed base
and branches
drooping at tips,
apical shoot erect

BARK
Reddish-brown,
fibrous and
shredding

TWIGS
Slender, densely
clothed with
scales, branching

LEAVES
Scale-like, ⅛in,
arranged in
flattened sprays,
in 4 rows,
pointed, resinous,
dark green with
whitish spots
below

CONES
Up to ½in,
elliptical, in erect
clusters, ripening
brown, cone
scales 10–12,
paired, with short
spine

This large attractive tree is found along the
Pacific coast from Alaska to California, where
it can be found growing alongside Giant
Sequoia (*Sequoiadendron giganteum*), and also
from Washington to Montana in the Rocky
Mountains. It is an important commercial tree,
both for its durable timber and for oil,
extracted from the leaf which is used for a
variety of purposes. It was previously used in
the construction of canoes and also for totem
poles.

YEW FAMILY, TAXACEAE

Western Yew
Taxus brevifolia

Evergreen
Up to 70ft

| J | F | M | A | M | J |
| J | A | S | O | N | D |

ID FACT FILE

CROWN
Conical

BARK
Reddish-brown,
scaly

TWIGS
Greenish-brown,
drooping

LEAVES
Needle-like,
½–1in, arranged
spirally but
flattened either
side of twig,
yellow-green,
with whitish
bands below

CONES
Males and
females on
separate trees,
males tiny,
yellow, solitary at
leaf base,
females up to
⅓in, fleshy,
scarlet cup,
surrounding
single brown seed

Western Yew is an understory tree of mixed coniferous forests with a range extending from Alaska south through Canada along the Pacific Coast to central California, and along the Rocky Mountains as far south as Idaho. It is found in a variety of habitats from canyon bottoms to upland sites on moist soils. All parts are poisonous but it is also the source of an anticancer drug. The wood is dense and durable, and valued for a wide variety of uses including cabinet making, and also canoe paddles.

YEW FAMILY, TAXACEAE

Evergreen
Up to 80ft

J	F	M	A	M	J
J	A	S	O	N	D

California Nutmeg
Torreya californica

ID FACT FILE

CROWN
Conical

BARK
Brown, shallowly
fissured, ridged
and scaly

TWIGS
Yellow-green,
becoming
reddish, usually
paired

LEAVES
Needle-like,
1–3in, in 2 rows,
pointed, shiny-
green above,
paler with two
whitish bands
below, aromatic

CONES
Males and
females on
separate trees,
males tiny,
yellow, at base of
needles, females
up to 1½in,
elliptical, solitary
at the ends of
twigs, fleshy
green marked
purple outer layer,
containing yellow-
brown, thick-
walled seed

Uncommon but not endangered, California
Nutmeg is found on the western slopes of the
Sierra Nevada in central California, and the
Coastal Ranges in the north. It is found in a
variety of plant communities, usually mixed
evergreen forests, in canyon bottoms but also
on exposed ridges, and usually between 3,000ft
and 6,000ft, although also at sea level. Like
many other coniferous trees of the west coast,
it will regenerate after fire. The aromatic and
good quality wood is not exploited due to the
relative rarity of the species.

MAGNOLIA FAMILY, MAGNOLIACEAE

Deciduous
Up to 150ft

J	F	M	A	M	J
J	A	S	O	N	D

Tulip Tree
Liriodendron tulipifera

ID FACT FILE

CROWN
Narrow, becoming spreading

BARK
Gray-brown, becoming thick and furrowed

TWIGS
Brown, hairless

LEAVES
Alternate, 3–6in, 4–6 spreading, paired lobes with the 2 at the apex only shallowly lobed so that the tip is a broad, notched, V-shape, dark shiny green above, paler below

FLOWERS
1½–2in, cup-shaped with 3 outer greenish petals and 6 inner petals, yellow and orange, solitary, erect

FRUITS
Narrow, conelike to 3in, brown

The Tulip Tree is a fast-growing, long-lived specimen tree favoring moist, well-drained soils and found usually as an isolated tree though sometimes in pure stands. It occurs naturally from Michigan and Vermont in the north, south to Florida and Louisiana, where it may be found at higher elevations. It is also widely grown ornamentally and is a valued timber tree. The common name refers to the flowers, which are tuliplike when young, although the foliage, the leaves of which look as though they have been cut at the tip, is also particularly impressive in autumn. In addition to being an attractive ornamental tree, the bark of this tall-growing native was also formerly exploited for medicinal purposes, and the durable wood was used for constructing canoes.

MAGNOLIA FAMILY, MAGNOLIACEAE

Southern Magnolia
Magnolia grandiflora

Evergreen
Up to 100ft

J	F	M	A	M	J
J	A	S	O	N	D

ID FACT FILE

CROWN
Conical,
branches
spreading

BARK
Gray, smooth,
becoming
furrowed and
scaly

TWIGS
Covered with
reddish hairs
when young

LEAVES
Alternate,
3¼–6½in,
elliptical, wavy-
edged, leathery,
shiny dark green
above, pale with
reddish hairs
below

FLOWERS
6–10in, solitary,
cup-shaped, white

FRUITS
2–2½in, conelike,
brown, covered
with reddish hairs

The Southern Magnolia is a large spreading evergreen tree naturally found from North Carolina to Florida and Texas in the west. Although sometimes taking many years to reach flowering size, it is now grown all over the world in temperate climes as a beautiful shade or ornamental tree, and there are several cultivated forms. It benefits from lustrous green foliage and a prolonged flowering season, the fragrant flowers appearing in spring and continuing throughout the summer.

LAUREL FAMILY, LAURACEAE

Evergreen
Up to 80ft

J	F	M	A	M	J
J	A	S	O	N	D

Californian Laurel
Umbellularia californica

ID FACT FILE

CROWN
Broadly rounded

BARK
Gray-brown,
smooth,
becoming
reddish-brown
and scaly

TWIGS
Greenish,
becoming
reddish-brown,
rounded, hairless

LEAVES
Alternate,
elliptical to
lanceolate, 3–5in,
leathery, shiny-
green above,
paler below

FLOWERS
Tiny, yellowish, in
small clusters in
the leaf axils

FRUITS
Up to 1¼in,
berrylike, yellow-
green ripening
purple-black, with
distinctive yellow
stem, in small
clusters,
enclosing single
brown nutlike
seed

An important tree both for local wildlife which
eat the seeds, and for people, Californian
Laurel is native to the Cascade and Coastal
Ranges of southern Oregon and California, and
it is also found throughout the Sierra Nevada
Mountains. It is a popular ornamental and
street tree and the wood is highly valued and
used in cabinet making, furniture and carving
among other things. The foliage, twigs, and
seeds are all highly aromatic when crushed and
used in cooking, and also medicinally.

PLANE FAMILY, PLATANACEAE

Deciduous
Up to 80ft

J	F	M	A	M	J
J	A	S	O	N	D

California Sycamore
Platanus racemosa

ID FACT FILE

CROWN
Irregular,
spreading

BARK
White, mottled
green and brown,
smooth,
becoming
furrowed at the
base

TWIGS
Pale brown, hairy
when young

LEAVES
Alternate,
3–10in, 3 or 5
narrow-lobed,
lobes pointed,
green, paler and
hairy below,
turning brown in
autumn

FLOWERS
Tiny, greenish, in
ball-like clusters,
males and
females in
separate clusters

FRUITS
1in, brown, 2–7
ball-like heads of
plumed seeds, in
pendent clusters

Despite having a restricted distribution, endemic to California, this species is relatively common in riparian woodlands. It is a commonly planted street and ornamental tree, and is also useful in erosion control. In the wild it is an important habitat tree in terms of maintaining the habitat in which it lives. With age it develops a distinctive leaning trunk and the mottled bark is also characteristic.

PLANE FAMILY, PLATANACEAE

Deciduous
Up to 80ft

J	F	M	A	M	J
J	A	S	O	N	D

Arizona Sycamore
Platanus wrightii

Arizona Sycamore is a large attractive tree and relatively common alongside rivers and streams in the canyons and foothills of Arizona and the extreme northwest of New Mexico. It also occurs in desert grasslands, where it makes a striking specimen. It is occasionally grown ornamentally although it tends to shed bark, twigs, leaves, and fruit. As with other sycamores, it is important in maintaining riparian habitats and is also used in erosion control.

ID FACT FILE

CROWN
Open, spreading

BARK
White, mottled green and brown, smooth, becoming furrowed at the base

TWIGS
Pale brown, hairy when young

LEAVES
Alternate, 6–10in, 3, 5 or 7 narrow-lobed, lobes pointed, green, paler and hairy below, turning brown in autumn

FLOWERS
Tiny, greenish, in ball-like clusters, males and females in separate clusters

FRUITS
1in, brown, 2–4 ball-like heads of plumed seeds, in pendent clusters

WITCH-HAZEL FAMILY, HAMAMELIDACEAE

Deciduous
Up to 100ft

J	F	M	A	M	J
J	A	S	O	N	D

Sweetgum
Liquidambar styraciflua

ID FACT FILE

CROWN
Conical

BARK
Gray-brown,
fissured

TWIGS
Brown, stout,
often with
corklike wings

LEAVES
Alternate, 3–6in,
star-shaped with
5–7 deep,
pointed lobes,
dark green
turning red,
purple and yellow
in autumn

FLOWERS
Tiny, greenish,
males in
clusters, females
in pendent
clusters on same
tree

FRUITS
1in, globose,
prickly, brown

An attractive widespread tree, Sweetgum is
common throughout eastern United States
from Conneticut to Florida and west to Texas
and Illinois. It also extends south into Mexico,
Guatemala, and Belize, where it is found at
high elevations. It is the source of an important
commercial timber called Satinwood, and also
"Storax"—a gum with medicinal properties. It
is now also widely grown ornamentally across
the United States, largely on account of its rich
autumn color.

Osage Orange
Maclura pomifera

ID FACT FILE

CROWN
Broad, rounded to irregular

BARK
Gray to brown, thick and furrowed into forking ridges

TWIGS
Brown, stout, with spines (or thorns) at nodes

LEAVES
Alternate, 2½–5in, oval, pointed at apex, shiny green above, paler below, turning yellow in autumn

FLOWERS
Tiny and inconspicuous, in dense clusters up to 1in, males and females on separate trees

FRUITS
4–5in, globular, fleshy ball, greenish-yellow

This utilitarian tree was originally found from Arkansas to Texas, but is now widely planted in eastern and northwestern states. Prior to the advent of barbed wire, it was much used in the Midwest for fencing because it has spines growing at nodes along the branches and shoots. A yellow dye can be extracted from the roots and the wood was previously used to construct bows, giving rise to the alternative common name, "Bowwood."

MULBERRY FAMILY, MORACEAE

White Mulberry
Morus alba

Deciduous
Up to 50ft

| J | F | M | A | M | J |
| J | A | S | O | N | D |

ID FACT FILE

CROWN
Narrow, rounded

BARK
Gray, smooth, becoming deeply ridged

TWIGS
Slender, hairy when young

LEAVES
Alternate, 2½–7in, oval, toothed, green above, paler and hairy below

FLOWERS
Tiny, greenish, in erect clusters, males and females on the same or separate trees

FRUITS
½–¾in, compound fruit, cylindrical, white, pink or purple, sweet-tasting

Originally native to China, this species was introduced to the United States and over several centuries has become naturalized in both eastern and western states. In its native habitat, the leaves are used as a foodstuff for silkworms in farms although in the United States it is primarily grown as an ornamental tree. Several cultivated forms exist, grown either for their flowers or habit. It is a common urban tree.

MULBERRY FAMILY, MORACEAE

Deciduous
Up to 60ft

J	F	M	A	M	J
J	A	S	O	N	D

Red Mulberry
Morus rubra

ID FACT FILE

CROWN
Broad, rounded

BARK
Reddish-brown, smooth with lenticels when young, becoming fissured and scaly

TWIGS
Brown, slender

LEAVES
Alternate, 4–8in, oval, long-pointed at apex, coarsely toothed, sometimes lobed, dull green above, hairy below, turning yellow in autumn

FLOWERS
Tiny, greenish, in erect clusters, males and females on the same or separate trees

FRUITS
1in, compound fruit, cylindrical, red or purple, sweet-tasting

An adaptable tree, Red Mulberry is found on prairies, in woodland, and along forest edges from Massachussets to Minnesota in the north, south to Texas and Florida; it is also cultivated in western states. The wood is weak but used locally for fenceposts and to an extent, furniture. The fruits are popular with birds and animals and people alike, but the species is very susceptible to a variety of diseases in cultivation.

ELM FAMILY, ULMACEAE

Netleaf Hackberry
Celtis reticulata

Deciduous
Up to 30ft

| J | F | M | A | M | J |
| J | A | S | O | N | D |

ID FACT FILE

CROWN
Spreading,
irregular

BARK
Gray, thick,
becoming warty
and scaly

TWIGS
Slender, reddish-
brown, usually
hairy though
sometimes
hairless

LEAVES
Alternate,
1¼–2½in, variably
lanceolate to
oval, pointed at
apex, unequal
base, green and
rough above,
paler and
distinctly veined
below

FLOWERS
Tiny, up to ⅛in,
males and
females both
greenish,
occurring at base
of young leaves

FRUITS
Up to ⅜in,
orange-red
drupe, sweet

Found in the southern central states of Kansas, Oklahoma, and Texas, and also ranging westward to southern California and Washington, this native hackberry favors moist sites although it can to an extent, also tolerate drought conditions. The common name derives from the fine netlike veination of the lower surface of the leaves, the upper surfaces of which are rough to the touch. The sweet fruits are much consumed by wildlife and were also formerly used by people as a food source.

ELM FAMILY, ULMACEAE

Deciduous
Up to 100ft

J	F	M	A	M	J
J	A	S	O	N	D

American Elm
Ulmus americana

This once common and abundant elm has a wide, predominantly eastern distribution, although it is found as far west as Montana and Wyoming, occurring roughly east of a line from eastern Montana to Texas. It also ranges across southeastern Canada. It has been very adversely affected by the introduction of Dutch Elm disease, which has wiped out both urban plantings and wild populations, although disease-resistant forms are now commercially available.

ID FACT FILE

CROWN
Broadly rounded, flat-topped

BARK
Gray, furrowed and ridged

TWIGS
Brown, hairless

LEAVES
Alternate, 3–6in, in 2 rows, oval, pointed, toothed, dark green and smooth above, paler and hairy below, turning yellow in autumn

FLOWERS
Appearing before the leaves, tiny, greenish, without petals, in clusters

FRUITS
Up to ½in, elliptical, flattened, reddish-brown, ciliate, with a narrow wing

WALNUT FAMILY, JUGLANDACEAE

Deciduous
Up to 30ft

J	F	M	A	M	J
J	A	S	O	N	D

Black Hickory
Carya texana

ID FACT FILE

CROWN
Irregular,
spreading

BARK
Dark gray, deeply
fissured

TWIGS
Brown, hairy
when young

LEAVES
Alternate,
pinnate, leaflets
usually 7, lance-
shaped, toothed,
up to 6in, shiny
green above,
paler and hairy
below

FLOWERS
Appearing before
the leaves,
greenish, males
in usually 3
drooping catkins
up to 3in,
females tiny at
tips of same
stalks

FRUITS
¾–1½in, rounded,
husk brown, with
4 unpronounced
wings splitting
to base, nuts
thick-shelled
containing edible
or sometimes
bitter seed

The westernmost
hickory species
found in North
America, Black
Hickory ranges
west of the
Mississippi River
from southern
Indiana as far
southwest as south-
central Texas. It is
most commonly seen
as a component of
oak woodland on dry, rocky
or sandy uplands. It is
occasionally grown as an ornamental tree but
otherwise is of little commercial importance
due to its relatively small size. The dense
wood, however, is a useful fuel-source.
Although the seeds are edible, they are rather
small and thick-shelled.

WALNUT FAMILY, JUGLANDACEAE

Deciduous
Up to 70ft

J	F	M	A	M	J
J	A	S	O	N	D

ID FACT FILE

CROWN
Open, broad

BARK
Gray-brown,
becoming
furrowed

TWIGS
Brown, stout

LEAVES
Alternate, pinnate
with 15–19
leaflets each
2½–4in long,
elliptical, finely
toothed, green
above, paler and
softly hairy below,
turning yellow in
autumn

FLOWERS
Small, greenish,
males in catkins,
pendent, 3–5in,
females in small
clusters at tips
of same twig

FRUITS
1–2in, egg-
shaped in small
clusters, husk
fleshy, smooth,
brown, containing
wrinkled, brown
nut

Northern California Walnut

Juglans hindsii

Found in similar habitats to *Juglans californica*, this species is restricted to central California. It has become naturalized through human association, hence its original range is uncertain. It is sometimes considered as a variety of its southern relative but is larger and also has larger leaflets and larger fruits, and the bark tends to be paler. It is sometimes planted as a street tree.

WALNUT FAMILY, JUGLANDACEAE

Deciduous
Up to 50ft

| J | F | M | A | M | J |
| J | A | S | O | N | D |

Arizona Walnut
Juglans major

ID FACT FILE

CROWN
Rounded, spreading

BARK
Gray-brown, becoming furrowed

TWIGS
Brown, stout

LEAVES
Alternate, pinnate with 9–13 leaflets each 2–4in long, elliptical, finely toothed, hairy when young, yellow-green

FLOWERS
Small, greenish, males in catkins, pendent, 3–5in, females in small clusters at tips of same twig

FRUITS
¾–1½in, egg-shaped in small clusters, husk fleshy, hairy, brown, containing wrinkled, brown nut

In scattered, localized populations, Arizona Walnut is found from central Texas west through New Mexico (and Mexico), to Arizona in a wide variety of habitats. Although the wood produced is high quality and used in the same ways as Black Hickory, the restricted distribution of this species means it is not widely used. The nuts are an important food source for animals such as squirrels.

WALNUT FAMILY, JUGLANDACEAE

Deciduous
Up to 30ft

J	F	M	A	M	J
J	A	S	O	N	D

Little Walnut

Juglans microcarpa

ID FACT FILE

CROWN
Broad, rounded

BARK
Gray, darkening
with age and
becoming
furrowed

TWIGS
Greenish-brown,
with brownish
hairy buds

LEAVES
Alternate,
pinnate with
7–13 (or more)
leaflets each
2–3in long, finely
toothed,
aromatic, yellow-
green above,
paler below,
turning yellow in
autumn

FLOWERS
Small, greenish,
males in catkins,
pendent, 2–4in,
females in
clusters of 6–8
at tips of same
twig

FRUITS
½–¾in, egg-
shaped in
clusters, husk
thin with rust-
colored hairs,
containing
wrinkled, brown
nut

This walnut is native to the south-central states of Kansas, New Mexico, and Texas, where it is found growing in rocky streambeds and valleys, and on low foothills. The common name derives from the characteristically small nuts, which are only ¾in in diameter at their largest. They are an important food source for many small animals. In common with other walnuts, this species produces chemicals to inhibit the growth of other competitive species and the wood is also used as a veneer. Hybridization between this species and *J. nigra* (Black Walnut), and *J. major* (Arizona Walnut) has been reported leading to specimens with larger leaflets.

BEECH FAMILY, FAGACEAE

Evergreen
Up to 100ft

J	F	M	A	M	J
J	A	S	O	N	D

Giant Chinkapin
Chrysolepis chrysophylla

ID FACT FILE

CROWN
Conical to
broadly rounded

BARK
Gray, smooth,
becoming
reddish-brown
and fissured into
plates

TWIGS
Gray, hairy when
young

LEAVES
Alternate, 2–5in,
lance-shaped,
leathery, shiny
dark green
above, golden-
yellow below

FLOWERS
Tiny, whitish,
males in erect
catkins up to
2½in at ends of
twigs, females at
base of male
catkins

FRUITS
Up to 1½in, a bur,
husk spiny, nuts
1–2, rounded,
brown, edible

An interesting and attractive species, Giant
Chinkapin is found throughout the Pacific
Coastal Ranges from Washington to central
California. In the north of its range it can be
found as a large tree growing with conifer
species, whereas in the south it tends to be a
shrubby understory species. It is long-lived and
able to rejuvenate from the base after fire or
wind damage. The wood is durable but the
species is not found in sufficient quantities to
facilitate commercial harvesting. The
chestnutlike fruits, which are sporadically
produced, are consumed by local wildlife.

BEECH FAMILY, FAGACEAE

Evergreen
Up to 80ft

J	F	M	A	M	J
J	A	S	O	N	D

Tanoak

Lithocarpus densiflorus

ID FACT FILE

CROWN
Conical

BARK
Brown, smooth
becoming
furrowed

TWIGS
Gray-brown,
sometimes hairy

LEAVES
Alternate, 2½–5in,
oblong, leathery,
wavy-toothed,
shiny green, with
glands above,
whitish-hairy
below when
young

FLOWERS
Tiny, white,
males in erect
catkins up to
4in, females tiny,
green, at base of
male catkins

FRUITS
1in, egg-shaped
acorn, yellow-
brown, bristly,
maturing in
second year

Restricted to the west of the United States,
Tanoak is only found from Oregon south along
the Cascades to California and in the Sierra
Nevada Mountains, where it grows in mixed
evergreen and oak forests. Although the fruits of
this species, the acorns, resemble those of oak
species, the flowers are similar to those of the
chestnuts. In the past this tree was an important
source of tannins and the acorns, once leached,
were ground to provide flour for baking.

BEECH FAMILY, FAGACEAE

Evergreen
Up to 80ft

J	F	M	A	M	J
J	A	S	O	N	D

Coast Live Oak
Quercus agrifolia

ID FACT FILE

CROWN
Rounded, spreading

BARK
Gray-brown, smooth, darkening with age and becoming ridged

TWIGS
Gray-brown, slender, hairy when young, with reddish-brown rounded buds at the tip

LEAVES
Alternate, 1¼–2½in, elliptical, spiny-edged, hollylike, thick, shiny-green above, paler and often hairy below

FLOWERS
Tiny, inconspicuous, without petals, males in pendulous clusters, females solitary or in small clusters

FRUITS
Acorn to 1½in, elongated, egg-shaped, cup deep, third the length of acorn, scales hairy, brown

Coast Live Oak is relatively common within its range. It is a drought-resistant tree found along the coast of central and southern California in the foothills of the Coastal Ranges. It is relatively long-lived (to 300 years) and forms quite gnarled aged specimens. The acorns are a staple food for squirrels and woodpeckers and the seeds were also formerly ground to provide a meal for cooking after leaching.

BEECH FAMILY, FAGACEAE

Evergreen
Up to 60ft

J	F	M	A	M	J
J	A	S	O	N	D

Arizona White Oak

Quercus arizonica

ID FACT FILE

CROWN
Irregular,
spreading

BARK
Pale gray,
becoming thick
and fissured

TWIGS
Brown, hairy,
with pointed
buds clustered at
the tip

LEAVES
Alternate,
1¼–3¼in,
elliptical to
oblong, toothed,
dull green above,
paler and hairy
below

FLOWERS
Tiny,
inconspicuous,
without petals,
males in
pendulous
clusters, females
solitary or in
small clusters,
males and
females in
separate clusters

FRUITS
Acorn to 1¼in,
egg-shaped, cup
deep, third the
length of acorn,
scales hairy and
warty, brown

Found in mixed oak and pinyon woodlands in the Trans Pecos range of Texas and also in New Mexico and Arizona, Arizona White Oak is a small, handsome evergreen or semi-evergreen species. It is known to readily hybridize with other species such as the Gray Oak (*Q. grisea*), which can make field identification difficult where the two species are found together. It is sometimes used for fuel wood.

BEECH FAMILY, FAGACEAE

Evergreen
Up to 100ft

| J | F | M | A | M | J |
| J | A | S | O | N | D |

Canyon Live Oak
Quercus chrysolepis

ID FACT FILE

CROWN
Rounded

BARK
Gray, darkening and becoming furrowed and ridged

TWIGS
Brown, hairy when young

LEAVES
Alternate, ¾–3¼in, oblong, spiny, leathery, shiny green above, paler below

FLOWERS
Tiny, inconspicuous, without petals, males in pendulous clusters, females solitary or in small clusters, males and females in separate clusters

FRUITS
Acorn to 2in, egg-shaped, cup shallow, third the length of acorn, scales densely yellow-hairy

Restricted to the Coastal Ranges of Oregon and California and the Sierra Nevada, with isolated scattered populations in Nevada and Arizona, this species is a canyon tree found in a wide variety of plant communities. It is found in pure stands and in mixed woodland, often on extreme slopes. It is occasionally planted as an ornamental tree for its broad evergreen habit, and the dense wood was formerly much exploited for a variety of uses.

BEECH FAMILY, FAGACEAE

Deciduous
Up to 60ft

J	F	M	A	M	J
J	A	S	O	N	D

Blue Oak
Quercus douglasii

Blue Oak is a relatively short-lived oak species, to only about 100 years, but forms part of the ancient oak forests of California, to which it is endemic. It is found on the lower slopes of the Coastal Ranges and west-facing foothills of the Sierra Nevada, in a variety of forest types, and also in pure stands. It is generally easily recognizable by the distinctive blue-green foliage. It is adapted to fire, having the ability to regenerate, and will also shed its leaves in harsh, dry periods as a further adaptation to the habitat in which it is found. Sometimes used as an ornamental tree or for fuel wood, it is also an important habitat tree much exploited by wildlife.

ID FACT FILE

CROWN
Irregular, spreading

BARK
Gray, shallowly fissured

TWIGS
Gray, brittle

LEAVES
Alternate, ¾–2½in, oblong, usually irregularly and shallowly 4–5 lobed, blue-green above, pale green below

FLOWERS
Tiny, inconspicuous, without petals, males in pendulous clusters, females solitary or in small clusters, males and females in separate clusters

FRUITS
Acorn to 1½in, elliptical, cup shallow, quarter the length of acorn, scales warty, brown

BEECH FAMILY, FAGACEAE

Coastal Sage Scrub Oak

Quercus dumosa

J	F	M	A	M	J
J	A	S	O	N	D

ID FACT FILE

CROWN
Rounded

BARK
Gray, becoming scaly

TWIGS
Gray-brown, hairy when young, with reddish-brown buds

LEAVES
Alternate, 1in, oblong, usually shallowly 3–9-lobed, lobes sometimes spiny-toothed, green above, paler and hairy below

FLOWERS
Tiny, inconspicuous, without petals, males in pendulous clusters, females solitary or in small clusters, males and females in separate clusters

FRUITS
Acorn to 1¼in, egg-shaped, cup deep, third the length of acorn, scales hairy, warty, brown

A rare, small tree, sometimes thicket-forming and shrublike, Coastal Sage Scrub Oak was once thought to be far more extensive. Recent research, however, has resulted in the majority of populations being reclassified as other, distinctive, scrub oak species. It is found in coastal scrubland on west-facing slopes in southern California (and also Baja California) at low elevations in small populations. It continues to be threatened largely due to urban pressures on its native habitat.

BEECH FAMILY, FAGACEAE

Deciduous
Up to 70ft

| J | F | M | A | M | J |
| J | A | S | O | N | D |

ID FACT FILE

CROWN
Rounded

BARK
Gray, darkening
with age,
becoming thick
and furrowed

TWIGS
Reddish-brown,
hairy when
young, with scaly
buds clustered at
ends of twigs

LEAVES
Alternate, 3–6in,
oblong, usually
deeply 5–9-lobed,
shiny green
above, paler and
hairy below,
turning red and
yellow in autumn

FLOWERS
Tiny,
inconspicuous,
without petals,
males in
pendulous
clusters, females
solitary or in
small clusters

FRUITS
Acorn to 1¼in,
egg-shaped, cup
shallow, third or
quarter the length
of acorn, scales
warty, brown

Gambel Oak

Quercus gambelii

This is a common oak within its range, especially in the southern Rocky Mountains, where it is found growing on slopes and in valleys up to 10,000ft, often in dense, pure stands. Ranging from southern Wyoming in the north, south to Arizona, New Mexico, Oklahoma, and Texas, Gambel Oak populations look particularly impressive in the autumn, exhibiting a range of autumn color. Both the foliage and acorns are browsed by wildlife such as deer and squirrels.

BEECH FAMILY, FAGACEAE

Deciduous
Up to 70ft

J	F	M	A	M	J
J	A	S	O	N	D

Oregon White Oak
Quercus garryana

ID FACT FILE

CROWN
Rounded

BARK
Gray, becoming
furrowed and
ridged

TWIGS
Reddish-brown,
hairy when
young, with
densely hairy,
scaly buds

LEAVES
Alternate, 3–6in,
elliptical, usually
deeply 5–9-
lobed, leathery,
shiny green
above, paler and
hairy below

FLOWERS
Tiny,
inconspicuous,
without petals,
males in
pendulous
clusters, females
solitary or in
small clusters,
males and
females in
separate clusters

FRUITS
Acorn to 1¼in,
egg-shaped, cup
shallow, third the
length of acorn,
scales warty,
brown

The northernmost of the western oaks,
Quercus garryana ranges from British
Columbia in the north, through Washington
and Oregon to the Coastal Ranges and Sierra
Nevada of California. It grows in a wide variety
of habitats and communities including
coniferous forests. It is a long-lived tree and
most successful as a canopy tree
on fire disturbed sites.
However, due to the
suppression of forest
fires within its range, it is
thought to be in decline.
It is a commercial timber
tree being used for fuel,
furniture and shipbuilding. As with
all oaks, the acorns are consumed
by a wide variety of wildlife.

Deciduous or
Semi-Evergreen
Up to 65ft

BEECH FAMILY, FAGACEAE

| J | F | M | A | M | J |
| J | A | S | O | N | D |

Gray Oak
Quercus grisea

ID FACT FILE

CROWN
Irregular

BARK
Gray, fissured

TWIGS
Reddish-brown,
finely gray-hairy,
with pointed
reddish-brown
buds clustered at
ends of twigs

LEAVES
Alternate, 1–3in,
elliptical,
rounded at base,
leathery, gray-
green above,
paler and hairy
below

FLOWERS
Usually
appearing with
the leaves, tiny,
inconspicuous,
without petals,
males in
pendulous
clusters, females
solitary or in
small clusters,
males and
females in
separate clusters

FRUITS
Acorn to ⅝in,
rounded, cup
deep, half the
length of acorn,
scales thin,
brown, hairy

Sometimes low-growing and shrublike, Gray
Oak is found along rocky slopes in the foothills
and canyons of Arizona east to western Texas.
It tends to be drought-deciduous and given
enough water, will retain its
leaves throughout winter
until the new foliage
emerges in the spring.
It is related to other
southwestern live oaks
such as *Quercus arizonica*,
with which it is often found
growing, either as a colonizing
tree several years after fire, or as
an understory or, less commonly, a
climax tree.

Deciduous
Up to 100ft

| J | F | M | A | M | J |
| J | A | S | O | N | D |

BEECH FAMILY, FAGACEAE

California Oak
Quercus lobata

ID FACT FILE

CROWN
Open, broadly spreading

BARK
Gray-black, deeply furrowed and ridged

TWIGS
Gray-brown, hairy when young

LEAVES
Alternate, 2½–5in, elliptical, deeply 9–11-lobed, lobes rounded, dull green and sometimes hairy above, paler and hairy below

FLOWERS
Tiny, inconspicuous, without petals, males in pendulous clusters, females solitary or in small clusters, males and females in separate clusters

FRUITS
Acorn to 2in, conical, cup deep, third the length of acorn, scales warty, brown

One of the tallest of the North American oak species, California Oak, also known as Valley Oak, is found throughout the valleys of central California and foothills of the Coastal Ranges and Sierra Nevada. Often dominant where it occurs, otherwise associating with other oak and pine species, it is a component of a critical habitat, home to several endangered species of animal. The wood has been used to an extent for cabinet-making, and previously for fuel wood, and the acorns were also once harvested for roasting.

BEECH FAMILY, FAGACEAE

Deciduous
Up to 80ft

J	F	M	A	M	J
J	A	S	O	N	D

Chinkapin Oak
Quercus muehlenbergii

ID FACT FILE

CROWN
Irregular

BARK
Pale gray,
fissured and
scaly

TWIGS
Brown, with
pointed buds
clustered at the
ends of twigs

LEAVES
Alternate, 5–8in,
elliptical,
coarsely toothed,
teeth gland-
tipped, shiny
green above,
paler below,
turning yellow or
red in autumn

FLOWERS
Usually
appearing with
the leaves, tiny,
inconspicuous,
without petals,
males in
pendulous
clusters, females
solitary or in
small clusters,
males and
females in
separate clusters

FRUITS
Acorn to 1¼in,
oval, cup deep,
third the length
of acorn, scales
ragged, hairy,
brown

A large, attractive tree, Chinkapin Oak is widely distributed from Vermont to Wisconsin, south through Iowa to Texas and New Mexico, and east to Florida, but notably absent from the Atlantic and Gulf coasts. It is usually found on upland rocky limestone soils, where it tends to dominate along with other hardwood species. It is a useful ornamental tree where its size can be accommodated, and the wood is also used for cabinet making and furniture.

BEECH FAMILY, FAGACEAE

Deciduous
Up to 100ft

Water Oak
Quercus nigra

ID FACT FILE

CROWN
Conical or
rounded

BARK
Dark gray,
smooth, darken-
ing and becoming
fissured and
ridged

TWIGS
Twigs and
pointed buds
reddish-brown

LEAVES
Alternate, 2½–5in,
variable, spat-
hulate to obovate,
tip sometimes 3-
lobed, blue-green
above, paler
below, turning
red, yellow and
brown in autumn

FLOWERS
Tiny,
inconspicuous,
without petals,
males in
pendulous
clusters, females
solitary or in
small clusters

FRUITS
Acorn to ¾in,
rounded, cup
shallow, third the
length of acorn,
scales
overlapping,
brown, maturing
in second year

Water Oak is found along the eastern coastal
plains from New Jersey to Florida, and west to
Texas, and ranging north along the Mississippi
River to Missouri. It is a
wetland species being found
in floodplains, along rivers,
and the edges of swamps.
Consequently it is only
occasionally grown as an
ornamental tree on suitable
soils, and the wood is not
highly valued.

BEECH FAMILY, FAGACEAE

Evergreen
Up to 20ft

| J | F | M | A | M | J |
| J | A | S | O | N | D |

Sandpaper Oak
Quercus pungens

ID FACT FILE

CROWN
Open

BARK
Grayish-brown,
furrowed and
ridged

TWIGS
Slender, with
rounded buds at
the tip

LEAVES
Alternate, 1–2in,
elliptical, lobed
and sharply
toothed, pointed
at tip, shiny
green and rough
above, paler and
grayish-hairy
below

FLOWERS
Tiny,
inconspicuous,
without petals,
males in
pendulous
clusters, females
solitary or in
small clusters,
males and
females in
separate clusters

FRUITS
Acorn to ⅝in,
oblong, cup third
the length of
acorn, scales
becoming brown
when mature

This small, often shrublike oak species is native to the Edwards Plateau of central Texas, although it is also found as far west as eastern Arizona and also in northern Mexico. A native of dry rocky limestone soils, Sandpaper Oak is usually found growing with other oaks and pinyon species. In common with other oak species, the seeds are sometimes used as a food source once the tannins have been leached out, and the roasted seed of this species are also sometimes used as a coffee substitute. The common name derives from the leaves, the upper surface of which have a roughish feel.

BEECH FAMILY, FAGACEAE

Evergreen
Up to 70ft

J	F	M	A	M	J
J	A	S	O	N	D

Interior Live Oak
Quercus wislizeni

ID FACT FILE

CROWN
Broad, rounded

BARK
Gray, smooth, becoming deeply furrowed and ridged

TWIGS
Greenish-brown, hairy when young, with orange-brown, pointed buds

LEAVES
Alternate, 1¼–2½in, oblong, leathery, with several sharp-pointed teeth, shiny green above, paler below

FLOWERS
Usually appearing with the leaves, tiny, inconspicuous, without petals, males in pendulous clusters, females solitary or in small clusters

FRUITS
Acorn to 1¼in, conical, pointed at tip, cup deep, half the length of acorn, scales overlapping, brown, maturing in second year

This western evergreen species of oak is related to Coast Live Oak but has paler bark and is smaller in size. Interior Live Oak also has a somewhat wider distribution, being found in the foothills of the Sierra Nevada as well as the Coastal Ranges. It is endemic to California and Baja California and is usually found on rocky slopes and in canyons in mixed oak and conifer forests. Two varieties are currently recognized, a shrubby form and a tree form, and the latter is often planted ornamentally.

BIRCH FAMILY, BETULACEAE

Deciduous
Up to 20ft

J	F	M	A	M	J
J	A	S	O	N	D

Speckled Alder
Alnus incana

ID FACT FILE

CROWN
Irregular

BARK
Gray, smooth
with conspicuous
lenticels

TWIGS
Gray-brown, hairy
when young

LEAVES
Alternate, 2–4in,
elliptical,
irregularly
double-toothed,
dull dark green
above, pale gray-
green with soft
hairs below

FLOWERS
Appearing before
the leaves, male
catkins yellow,
drooping,
1½–3in, females
reddish, ovoid,
0.5cm

FRUITS
Woody, conelike,
½in on short
stalks, enclosing
rounded flat
nutlets

A small tree (sometimes a shrub), Speckled
Alder is widespread across Canada almost to
Alaska, and found in the United States south to
Virginia and west to Iowa at altitudes almost at
the timber line. It is a short-lived species but
not without benefits. Like all
alders, its roots have nitrogen-
fixing properties and it is also
used in watershed management,
as well as being an important
forage tree for wildlife.

BIRCH FAMILY, BETULACEAE

Deciduous
Up to 80ft

J	F	M	A	M	J
J	A	S	O	N	D

Arizona Alder
Alnus oblongifolia

ID FACT FILE

CROWN
Rounded

BARK
Gray, smooth,
becoming
fissured

TWIGS
Slender, hairy
when young

LEAVES
Alternate,
1½–3¼in,
elliptical, double-
toothed, dark
green above,
pale green and
often hairy below

FLOWERS
Appearing before
the leaves, male
catkins yellow,
drooping,
2–3¼in, females
reddish, ovoid,
¼in

FRUITS
Woody, conelike,
½–¾in, in
clusters on short
stalks, with black
scales, enclosing
small, rounded
flat nutlets

Like all alders, this species has the ability to fix
nitrogen from the soil, which consequently
means they are used for wetland restoration
(where they both stabilize and enrich soil
conditions). Arizona Alder is a
relatively large and handsome
species normally found in
moist locations in the canyons
and mountainsides of New
Mexico and Arizona. This
species is not widely grown
ornamentally although the
timber is used to some
extent as firewood.

BIRCH FAMILY, BETULACEAE

Deciduous
Up to 80ft

White Alder
Alnus rhombifolia

ID FACT FILE

CROWN
Rounded, open

BARK
Gray, smooth, becoming brown and fissured

TWIGS
Slender, hairy when young

LEAVES
Alternate, 2–4in, elliptical, double-toothed, dark green above, pale green and slightly hairy below

FLOWERS
Appearing before the leaves, male catkins yellow, drooping, 1½–5in, females reddish, ovoid, 1cm

FRUITS
Woody, conelike, ½–¾in, in clusters on short stalks, with black scales, enclosing small, rounded flat nutlets

The only species of alder native to California, White Alder has an extensive range albeit restricted to riparian habitats alongside streams. It is found from Washington and Idaho south to Nevada and California. Of some use as a fuel wood and occasionally planted as an ornamental tree, the main use of this species is in reforesting disturbed wetland habitats where it quickly establishes itself.

BIRCH FAMILY, BETULACEAE

Red Alder
Alnus rubra

ID FACT FILE

CROWN
Rounded

BARK
Mottled gray-white, smooth

TWIGS
Green, with gray hairs when young

LEAVES
Alternate, 3–6in, oval to elliptical with double-toothed margins, dark green above, pale green and hairy below

FLOWERS
Catkins appear before leaves, males yellow, drooping, 4–6in, females reddish, ovoid, ⅜in

FRUITS
Woody, conelike, ½–1¼in on short stalks containing flat winged nutlets

Deciduous
Up to 100ft

J	F	M	A	M	J
J	A	S	O	N	D

Found from Alaska south to California on the Pacific Northwest coast, Red Alder favors moist, well-drained sandy or gravel loam soils. It forms pioneer thickets on disturbed sites but is soon overtaken by the coniferous understory. However, it can persist and form pure stands in riparian habitats. It is an important commercial hardwood with a variety of uses.

BIRCH FAMILY, BETULACEAE

Deciduous
Up to 30ft

J	F	M	A	M	J
J	A	S	O	N	D

Mountain Alder
Alnus tenuifolia

ID FACT FILE

CROWN
Rounded

BARK
Gray, smooth
becoming brown
and scaly

TWIGS
Slender, reddish
and hairy when
young

LEAVES
Alternate, 1½–4in,
elliptical, lobed,
double-toothed,
dark green above,
yellow-green and
sometimes hairy
below

FLOWERS
Appearing before
the leaves, male
catkins yellow,
drooping, 1–3in,
females brown,
narrowly ovoid,
¼in

FRUITS
Woody, conelike,
½–⅝in, in
clusters on short
stalks, with black
scales, enclosing
small, rounded
flat nutlets

Mountain Alder is a small tree, which in disturbed sites or where browsed, has the alder tendency to become shrublike. It is found from Alaska southeast to California and also throughout the Rockies south to New Mexico alongside streams and other wet sites where it is locally common. A red dye was previously extracted from the ground bark of this tree. Often treated as a subspecies of *A. incana*.

BIRCH FAMILY, BETULACEAE

Deciduous
Up to 27ft

J	F	M	A	M	J
J	A	S	O	N	D

Water Birch
Betula occidentalis

ID FACT FILE

CROWN
Rounded,
spreading

BARK
Reddish-brown,
shiny, with thin
horizontal lines

TWIGS
Green, slender

LEAVES
Alternate, 1–2in,
ovate, double-
toothed, green
above, yellow-
green below,
turning yellow in
autumn

FLOWERS
Tiny, males
yellowish in
drooping catkins
up to 4in,
females greenish
in erect catkins
up to 1½in, in
separate clusters
on the same twig

FRUIT
conelike,
brownish up to
1¼in, with many
tiny winged
nutlets

Water Birch is a small tree with a tendency to
sucker and form small thickets. It is relatively
widespread throughout the western states but
is uncommon and localized where it occurs. It
is found as far south as California and New
Mexico and just creeps into the states of North
and South Dakota and Nebraska in the
extreme east of its range. It is tolerant of
flooding with a fibrous root system and
consequently, like River Birch, is of use in
erosion control especially in wet areas.

BIRCH FAMILY, BETULACEAE

Deciduous
Up to 90ft

J	F	M	A	M	J
J	A	S	O	N	D

Paper Birch
Betula papyrifera

ID FACT FILE

CROWN
Erect, becoming
open and
spreading

BARK
White, peeling off
in papery strips
to reveal orange
inner bark, with
horizontal gray
lenticels

TWIGS
Reddish-brown

LEAVES
Alternate,
1½–4in, oval,
pointed at apex,
double-toothed,
dull green above,
pale green
below, turning
yellow in autumn

FLOWERS
Tiny, males
yellowish in
drooping catkins
up to 4in,
females greenish
in erect catkins
up to 1½in, in
separate clusters
on the same twig

FRUIT
Conelike,
brownish up to
2in, with many
tiny winged
nutlets

Found at altitudes up to 4,000ft across the
United States from New York and North
Carolina to Oregon and Colarado, Paper
Birch has a long history of human association.
The peeling bark was previously used in the
construction of canoes and the
wood is a valuable timber. It
also plays an important
ecological role, being a food
source for various woodland
mammals and birds.

BIRCH FAMILY, BETULACEAE

Deciduous
Up to 30ft

| J | F | M | A | M | J |
| J | A | S | O | N | D |

Western Hophornbeam
Ostrya knowltonii

This species is found only in moist, canyon bottoms of semidesert in southeast Utah and northern Arizona, including the Grand Canyon, where it grows with oaks and various pine species. The fruits give it its common name as they resemble those of hops (*Humulus* sp.), and the strength of the hard dense wood is reflected in the name *Ostrya*, meaning hardwood tree.

ID FACT FILE

CROWN
Narrowly rounded

BARK
Gray, shallowly fissured and shredding

TWIGS
Green, hairy when young

LEAVES
Alternate, ¾–2½in, oval, toothed, yellow-green, hairy

FLOWERS
Appearing before the leaves, tiny, inconspicuous, greenish, males in pendant catkins, forming over winter, females in smaller catkins at the ends of twigs

FRUITS
Up to 1½in, oval, conelike clusters of small nutlets, brown, papery

CACTUS FAMILY, CACTACEAE

Leafless Tree Cactus
Up to 33ft

J	F	M	A	M	J
J	A	S	O	N	D

Saguaro
Cereus giganteus

ID FACT FILE

HABIT
Columnar, with
spiny trunk and
erect spiny
branches

TRUNK & BRANCHES
Green, smooth
and waxy,
cylindrical, with
vertical ribs and
clusters of
spines up to 2in

WOOD
Pale brown,
vertical ribs,
surrounding inner
thick whitish
pith, inner tissue
fleshy

FLOWERS
Funnel-shaped,
up to 4in, creamy-
white with yellow
center, at ends of
branches,
opening at night

FRUITS
Up to 4in, egg-
shaped, red,
fleshy, spineless,
edible, with many
small brown
seeds

This seminal species is synonymous with the Sonoran Desert of southern California and Arizona, where it is found on rocky slopes often associated with Paloverde (*Cercidium* sp.). Now protected, it was previously widely used for its fruits and fibers. Like all cacti it is leafless, the stems possessing chlorophyll and taking over the role of photosynthesis. It is also able to absorb water through the shallow roots and store it in the succulent stems for when it is needed. Despite the thick, abundant spines, it is used by various birds, which make nesting holes in the stems. The seeds are also consumed in large quantities by avian fauna.

WILLOW FAMILY, SALICACEAE

White Poplar
Populus alba

Deciduous
Up to 80ft

J	F	M	A	M	J
J	A	S	O	N	D

ID FACT FILE

CROWN
Narrow, open

BARK
Gray, smooth, becoming furrowed with age

TWIGS
Brown, whitish-hairy when young

LEAVES
Alternate, 2–4in, oval, 3–5 lobed, gray-green above, densely whitish-hairy below, turning yellow or sometimes reddish in autumn

FLOWERS
Catkins up to 2½in, whitish-hairy, pendulous, males and females on separate trees

FRUITS
Up to ¼in, elliptical capsule, brown, splitting in 2 to release tiny cottony seeds

A distinctive poplar due to the characteristic leaves (white on the underside), *Populus alba* is originally native to southern Europe and Asia but was introduced to North America during Colonial times. It is widely grown and has become naturalized across much of the United States and southern Canada. It is an attractive and fast-growing ornamental tree, although its suckering habit can lead to it spreading to such an extent that it may become locally invasive. In common with species of willow, the bark of this tree contains chemicals used as the basis for non-synthetic aspirin. Various ornamental cultivars are now available in a range of forms.

WILLOW FAMILY, SALICACEAE

Deciduous
Up to 100ft

Narrowleaf Cottonwood
Populus angustifolia

ID FACT FILE

CROWN
Narrow, rounded

BARK
Gray-brown, becoming furrowed and ridged

TWIGS
Yellow-green, slender

LEAVES
Alternate, 3–4in, narrowly lance-shaped, pointed at tip, finely toothed, shiny green above, paler below, turning yellow in autumn

FLOWERS
Catkins up to 3¼in, reddish-brown, pendulous, males and females on separate trees

FRUITS
Up to ¼in, elliptical capsule, brown, splitting in 2 to release tiny cottony seeds

Easily distinguished by its especially narrow, willowlike leaves, this is the common cottonwood of the Rocky Mountains. It extends from western Canada south through the Rockies as far as Texas, California, and into Mexico. It is slow-growing and often smaller than the given height but is a successful colonizing tree important in areas subjected to occasional flooding. Consequently it is a useful species for erosion control and is also an important food source for many native animals and birds. The inner bark of the tree was also formerly used for medicinal properties.

WILLOW FAMILY, SALICACEAE

Deciduous
Up to 100ft

J	F	M	A	M	J
J	A	S	O	N	D

Balsam Poplar
Populus balsamifera

ID FACT FILE

CROWN
Narrow

BARK
Brown, smooth, becoming gray and furrowed into ridges

TWIGS
Brown, with sticky buds producing a yellow resin

LEAVES
Alternate, 3–5in, oval, pointed at tip, dark green above, paler below, hairless

FLOWERS
Catkins up to 4in, brown, pendulous, males and females on separate trees

FRUITS
Up to ½in, egg-shaped capsule, pointed at tip, brown, splitting in 2 to release tiny cottony seeds

One of the northernmost poplar species, this tree is found across the entire width of North America. In the United States it is found as far south as Pennsylvania and Iowa (with isolated localized populations also found in Virginia) and as far west as Colorado, although a subspecies (*Populus balsamifera* ssp. *trichocarpa*) is found in the extreme west from Alaska south to California and Utah. It is usually found alongside streams and lakes and is of some use in habitat stabilization in appropriate soil conditions.

WILLOW FAMILY, SALICACEAE

Deciduous
Up to 80ft

J	F	M	A	M	J
J	A	S	O	N	D

Fremont Cottonwood
Populus fremontii

ID FACT FILE

CROWN
Open, spreading

BARK
Gray, smooth, darkening and becoming furrowed with age

TWIGS
Green, with large terminal buds

LEAVES
Alternate, 2–3in, triangular, pointed at tip, finely toothed, pale green, turning yellow in autumn

FLOWERS
Catkins up to 3in, reddish-brown, pendulous, males and females on separate trees

FRUITS
Up to ½in, elliptical capsule, brown, splitting in 3 to release tiny cottony seeds

Native to the southwest, this species is related to Eastern Cottonwood (*P. deltoides*), and is similar in its requirements, although less dependent on actual flooding. Fremont Cottonwood is a short-lived riparian species and an indication of a permanent water supply where it grows, from Colorado to California in the west, and Texas in the southeast. It is found either in open groves alongside streams and rivers, or with other riparian trees such as willows and alders in similar habitats. The wood is used locally for fuel wood, pulp, and traditional carvings.

Deciduous
Up to 80ft

J	F	M	A	M	J
J	A	S	O	N	D

Quaking Aspen
Populus tremuloides

ID FACT FILE

CROWN
Narrowly rounded

BARK
Whitish-gray,
smooth,
darkening and
becoming
furrowed with age

TWIGS
Reddish-brown,
smooth

LEAVES
Alternate, 3–4in,
broadly oval,
pointed at apex,
rounded at base,
finely toothed, on
very slender
stalks, green
above, paler
below, turning
golden in autumn

FLOWERS
Catkins up to
2½in, reddish-
brown,
pendulous, males
and females on
separate trees

FRUITS
Up to ¼in,
elliptical capsule,
brown, splitting in
2 to release tiny
cottony seeds

The most widely distributed tree in the
northern hemisphere, Quaking Aspen is found
across Canada from Newfoundland to Alaska,
penetrating south along the Rocky Mountains
into New Mexico and Texas, where it is found
at elevations up to 10,000ft. In the east it is
found more or less east of a line from Minnesota
to Iowa. Like all aspens, it is fast-growing
and quick to colonize newly disturbed sites.
Quaking Aspen also spreads by suckering from
the roots, often forming large clonal colonies.
An important habitat tree, it is also planted
ornamentally and the wood has a range of uses.

WILLOW FAMILY, SALICACEAE

Deciduous
Up to 30ft

J	F	M	A	M	J
J	A	S	O	N	D

Feltleaf Willow
Salix alaxensis

ID FACT FILE

CROWN
Irregular,
spreading

BARK
Reddish-brown,
becoming
furrowed

TWIGS
Reddish-brown,
densely whitish-
hairy

LEAVES
Alternate, 2–4in,
elliptical, pointed,
dull green above,
densely whitish-
hairy below

FLOWERS
Usually appearing
before the
leaves, tiny, in
erect catkins to
3½in, stalkless,
brownish, males
and females on
separate trees

FRUITS
Up to ¼in, white
capsule, woolly

One of the northernmost willow species,
Feltleaf Willow is native to northwest Canada
and Alaska. It generally prefers rocky, gravelly
soils alongside rivers and streams where it
forms a small tree. However, it can also be
found up to, and beyond the timber line,
where it tends to be more thicket-forming and
shrubby. It is used for fuel wood and in the
far north, forms an important resource in this
respect, and is also browsed by animals such
as moose.

WILLOW FAMILY, SALICACEAE

Deciduous
Up to 60ft

J	F	M	A	M	J
J	A	S	O	N	D

Peachleaf Willow

Salix amygdaloides

In the United States, this small tree is found from New York southwest to Texas, spreading northwest through the Rocky Mountains to Montana and Idaho; it is also found across southern Canada. Peachleaf Willow is a wetland species found alongside streams and rivers, often growing with cottonwood species. Although it has a widespread range across North America, it is generally locally uncommon.

ID FACT FILE

CROWN
Irregular, spreading

BARK
Gray-brown, becoming scaly

TWIGS
Orange-brown, thin, flexible

LEAVES
Alternate, 2–4in, lance-shaped, narrowly pointed, finely toothed, shiny green above, densely whitish-hairy below

FLOWERS
Usually appearing before the leaves, tiny, in erect catkins to 3in, yellowish, males and females on separate trees

FRUITS
Up to ¼in, reddish-yellow, capsule

WILLOW FAMILY, SALICACEAE

Deciduous
Up to 20ft

| J | F | M | A | M | J |
| J | A | S | O | N | D |

Pussy Willow
Salix discolor

ID FACT FILE

CROWN
Rounded

BARK
Gray, fissured
and scaly

TWIGS
Reddish-brown,
hairy when young

LEAVES
Alternate, 1½–4in,
narrowly elliptical,
sometimes
irregularly
toothed, hairy
when young,
shiny green
above, gray or
whitish below

FLOWERS
Usually
appearing before
the leaves, tiny,
in erect catkins
to 2in, with silky
white hairs,
males showy,
yellowish, males
and females on
separate trees

FRUITS
Up to ½in, pale
brown, narrow,
hairy capsule

Pussy Willow is a colonizing species of wetlands, sometimes growing as a shrub, or as a small, multistemmed tree. It is native across southern Canada, and found in the United States from Maine south to Delaware and west to Missouri and Minnesota. Scattered populations are also found in North Dakota and Wyoming. An important habitat tree, it is often grown ornamentally for the showy flowers, and cut stems are harvested on a commercial basis in early spring and forced into flowering for the florist trade. The bark and roots, in common with other willow species, contain chemicals called "salicylates", which are the basis for aspirin.

WILLOW FAMILY, SALICACEAE

Deciduous
Up to 20ft

J	F	M	A	M	J
J	A	S	O	N	D

ID FACT FILE

CROWN
Irregular to
rounded

BARK
Gray, furrowed

TWIGS
Gray, densely
hairy when young

LEAVES
Alternate,
1½in–4in, linear,
densely gray-
hairy

FLOWERS
Usually
appearing after
the leaves, tiny,
in erect catkins
to 1½in, hairy,
yellowish, males
and females on
separate trees

FRUITS
Up to ¼in, pale
brown, narrow,
hairy capsule

Hinds Willow
Salix hindsiana

Restricted to wet sites alongside streams and
ditches, and often found on sandbars, this
willow is also known as Sandbar Willow. It has
a restricted range, from southern Oregon to
southern California and the Baja Peninsula,
and has formerly been treated as a variety of
the more shrubby, and more widespread
Narrowleaf Willow (*S. exigua*). It suckers
profusely and as a consequence, is useful in
soil stabilization, especially on riverbanks or
along ditches.

WILLOW FAMILY, SALICACEAE

Deciduous
Up to 50ft

J	F	M	A	M	J
J	A	S	O	N	D

Pacific Willow

Salix lasiandra

ID FACT FILE

CROWN
Open, irregular

BARK
Gray, furrowed
and scaly

TWIGS
Orange-brown

LEAVES
Alternate, 2–5in,
narrowly lance-
shaped, finely-
toothed, shiny
green above,
whitish below

FLOWERS
Usually
appearing with
the leaves, tiny,
in erect catkins
to 4in, hairy,
yellowish, males
and females on
separate trees

FRUITS
Up to ¼in,
reddish-brown,
narrow, capsule

Pacific Willow is a common willow of the northwest and found from Alaska south through western Canada along the Rockies and Coastal Ranges to New Mexico and California. Both the flexible stems and bark have been used in basket weaving, and the wood has also been used for charcoal. This moisture-loving species is found along streams and lakes and is sometimes considered as a subspecies of the eastern Shining Willow (*S. lucida*). Like many willows, it is both a valued wildlife tree and also important in erosion control.

WILLOW FAMILY, SALICACEAE

Deciduous
Up to 30ft

Arroyo Willow
Salix lasiolepis

Arroyo Willow is a variable species and may
grow as a thicket-forming shrub or as a small
graceful tree, and is found from Washington,
south through Idaho and Oregon, to California
and New Mexico. It is a riparian species
inhabiting wetland areas such as stream banks
and canyon gullies, where it is fast-growing but
short-lived. In common with other species of
willow, the stems are utilized for basket
weaving and it is sometimes coppiced to
provide suitable stems.

ID FACT FILE

CROWN
Irregular

BARK
Gray-brown,
darkening and
becoming
furrowed and
ridged

TWIGS
Yellow-brown,
hairy

LEAVES
Alternate, 2–4in,
narrowly lance-
shaped, finely
toothed, shiny
green above,
whitish below

FLOWERS
Usually
appearing with
the leaves, tiny,
in erect catkins
to 4in, hairy,
yellowish, males
and females on
separate trees

FRUITS
Up to ¼in,
reddish-brown,
narrow, capsule

WILLOW FAMILY, SALICACEAE

Deciduous
Up to 100ft

| J | F | M | A | M | J |
| J | A | S | O | N | D |

Black Willow
Salix nigra

ID FACT FILE

CROWN
Irregular,
spreading

BARK
Dark brown,
furrowed into
forking ridges

TWIGS
Orange-brown,
slender

LEAVES
Alternate, 3–5in,
narrowly lance-
shaped, long-
pointed, finely
toothed, dark
green above,
paler and often
hairy below,
turning yellow in
autumn

FLOWERS
Usually appearing
before the leaves,
tiny, in erect
catkins to 3in,
yellowish, males
and females in
separate clusters
at ends of twigs

FRUITS
Up to ¼in,
reddish-brown
capsule, hairless

A variable tree, but in parts of its range at least, it is the largest of the North American willows and the only one of significant importance. The wood is used for a variety of purposes and, because it roots so easily from cuttings, it is also very useful in preventing soil erosion. The bark and leaves were also formerly used for their medicinal properties. Black Willow is found from Maine south to Florida, and west to Texas and Minnesota, although it also occurs sporadically from western Texas to California.

HEATHER FAMILY, ERICACEAE

Evergreen
Up to 80ft

J	F	M	A	M	J
J	A	S	O	N	D

Pacific Madrone
Arbutus menziesii

ID FACT FILE

CROWN
Spreading

BARK
Red, smooth,
peeling off in
large, thin plates
revealing lighter
bark beneath

TWIGS
Green or pale
red, smooth,
turning reddish-
brown

LEAVES
Alternate, 2–4in,
elliptical,
occasionally
toothed, leathery,
glossy, dark
green above,
paler below

FLOWERS
Urn-shaped, ¼in,
white sometimes
tinged pink, in
terminal clusters
up to 6in

FRUITS
½in across,
globular, warty,
orange-red

A large attractive tree with peeling red bark, scented flowers, and bright attractive fruits, this tree is often used in ornamental landscaping. In its native habitat of the Pacific coastal region as far south as southern California and also in the Sierra Nevada, Pacific Madrone displays remarkable adaptations to its environment. The species is particularly adapted to fire, after which it will readily resprout, and the germination of seeds is also enhanced by the occurrence of fire. The fruits are especially popular with birds and squirrels, and contrast sharply against the glossy, evergreen foliage. It is usually smaller growing in cultivation.

HEATHER FAMILY, ERICACEAE

Evergreen
Up to 20ft

J	F	M	A	M	J
J	A	S	O	N	D

Texas Madrone
Arbutus xalapensis

ID FACT FILE

CROWN
Rounded

BARK
Gray or reddish-brown, smooth, peeling off in large, thin plates, revealing lighter bark beneath

TWIGS
Red, smooth, hairy when young, turning reddish-brown

LEAVES
Alternate, 2–4in, elliptical, leathery, glossy, dark green above, paler and hairy below

FLOWERS
Urn-shaped, ¼in, white sometimes tinged pink, in terminal clusters up to 6in

FRUITS
½in across, globular, warty, orange-red or yellow

Texas Madrone is an uncommon tree with a much wider distribution south of the United States in Mexico and Guatemala, but is nevertheless well known in south-central Texas and west to eastern New Mexico. It is found in dry, sunny canyons and on mountain slopes. Its smooth bark makes it an attractive ornamental tree. It is relatively slow growing and is found in drier areas than other madrone species. Many clusters of typically *Erica*-like flowers are produced in the spring. The wood is used in the making of various utensils, and the leaves and fruits provide a valuable food source for local wildlife.

ROSE FAMILY, ROSACEAE

Deciduous
Up to 30ft

J	F	M	A	M	J
J	A	S	O	N	D

Saskatoon Serviceberry
Amelanchier alnifolia

ID FACT FILE

CROWN
Spreading, irregular

BARK
Gray-brown, smooth, becoming fissured with age

TWIGS
Reddish, hairless

LEAVES
Alternate, 1¼–2½in, oval to rounded, toothed, dark green above, paler and sometimes hairy below

FLOWERS
Appearing with the leaves in erect terminal clusters, 1¼in, petals narrow, white

FRUITS
⅜in, purple, apple-like, edible

Although predominantly a western species—found from Alaska south along the Rockies and Coastal Ranges to Colorado and California respectively—*Amelanchier alnifolia* also ranges as far east as Manitoba (and locally, eastern Quebec) in Canada, and Minnesota in the United States. It is a relatively common tree of woodlands and clearings and the sweet fruits are eaten by people and wildlife. Although the species is not harvested commercially, its wood is strong and sometimes exploited for a range of uses, as are the young, willowlike branches.

ROSE FAMILY, ROSACEAE

Deciduous
Up to 30ft

J	F	M	A	M	J
J	A	S	O	N	D

Black Hawthorn
Crataegus douglasii

ID FACT FILE

CROWN
Broad, dense

BARK
Gray, scaly and rough

TWIGS
Red, slender, with curved spines, up to 1¼in

LEAVES
Alternate, shiny, 1¼–4in, oval, narrower at base, toothed, sometimes lobed, dark green, paler below

FLOWERS
⅜–½in across, white, with 3–5 styles, in broad clusters

FRUITS
⅜–½in, rounded, black, 3–5-seeded in drooping clusters

Black Hawthorn is a small tree with a tendency to become shrubby in exposed areas. It has a disjunct distribution, largely restricted to the west coast, from Alaska to California arching inland to Wyoming. Isolated populations are also known from Minnesota and Michigan, possibly due to previous human association. Its main use is in soil stabilization; otherwise its only real importance is its value to wildlife as a food plant, although it is sometimes grown as an ornamental tree.

ROSE FAMILY, ROSACEAE

Deciduous
Up to 60ft

| J | F | M | A | M | J |
| J | A | S | O | N | D |

Oneseed Hawthorn
Crataegus monogyna

ID FACT FILE

CROWN
Rounded, dense
to spreading

BARK
Gray to brown,
scaly

TWIGS
Slender, covered
in slender, red-
brown spines, up
to ⅝in

LEAVES
Alternate, shiny,
1–2in, ovate,
deeply 3–7-
lobed, dark green
above, paler
below

FLOWERS
⅜–⅝in across,
white or pink,
with a single
style, in flat
clusters

FRUITS
⅜–⅝in, rounded,
bright red with
a single seed

Often wrongly confused with English
Hawthorn (*C. oxyacantha*), this species, native
to, and long cultivated in Europe, reached
North America with the first Pioneers. It is
now escaped and widely naturalized.
Sometimes grown ornamentally with various
single and double-flowered varieties in a range
of colors, it is also an extremely useful hedging
plant if kept cut.

ROSE FAMILY, ROSACEAE

Deciduous
Up to 40ft

J	F	M	A	M	J
J	A	S	O	N	D

ID FACT FILE

CROWN
Open, irregular

BARK
Reddish-brown,
deeply fissured
and scaly

TWIGS
Reddish, hairy
when young,
sometimes spiny

LEAVES
Alternate,
1½–3in, oval,
finely toothed,
green above,
paler and hairy
below, turning
orange and red
in autumn

FLOWERS
Up to ¾in, in
clusters, petals
5, pink or white

FRUITS
Up to ¾in,
oblong, fleshy,
yellow to red

Western Oregon Crabapple
Malus fusca

The only western species of crabapple, Western Oregon Crabapple is found along the coast from Alaska to California, extending inland along streams and rivers. As with its eastern relatives the dense wood is worked into tool handles and the bark has medicinal properties. The fruit, an important natural food source, was also previously much used as it can be dried and used in preserves.

Deciduous
Up to 50ft

ROSE FAMILY, ROSACEAE

Cultivated Apple
Malus pumila

Of old hybrid origin, the Cultivated Apple
was introduced to the United States and
widely grown as an orchard tree for the
copious edible fruits it produces, used
for a range of drinks and foodstuffs. There
are thousands of cultivated forms and
varieties and it can often be found
naturalized in areas previously inhabited
by human populations.

ID FACT FILE

CROWN
Dense

BARK
Brown, fissured

TWIGS
Downy

LEAVES
Alternate,
1½–5in, elliptical,
toothed, dark
green, hairy
above, downy
below

FLOWERS
1in, in clusters,
petals 5, white
tinged with pink,
sepals hairy,
persistent

FRUITS
2–4in, fleshy,
sweet-tasting

ROSE FAMILY, ROSACEAE

Deciduous
Up to 50ft

| J | F | M | A | M | J |
| J | A | S | O | N | D |

Wild Apple
Malus sylvestris

Now naturalized locally across the United States, this is one of the parents of the Cultivated Apple (*M. pumila*). Formerly cultivated in its own right, the fruit is smaller and harder than that of the Cultivated Apple, and is also sour-tasting. Wild trees tend to be armed with spines and have pure white flowers, whereas those in cultivation tend to lose the spines and the flowers are always tinged with pink.

ID FACT FILE

CROWN
Dense

BARK
Gray, fissured becoming scaly

TWIGS
Downy when young, spiny

LEAVES
Alternate, 1¼–4½in, elliptical, toothed, dark green, hairless

FLOWERS
1in, in clusters, petals 5, white, sometimes tinged with pink, sepals hairy, persistent

FRUITS
1in, hard, sour

ROSE FAMILY, ROSACEAE

Deciduous
Up to 30ft

J	F	M	A	M	J
J	A	S	O	N	D

American Plum
Prunus americana

A small attractive tree, this species is widely grown for its fruit, for which a number of improved cultivated varieties have been developed. It is also grown as an ornamental tree for the attractive clusters of white flowers. It is native from New Hampshire south to Florida and west to Oklahoma and Montana, south of the Great Lakes.

ID FACT FILE

CROWN
Irregular, broad

BARK
Dark brown, scaly

TWIGS
Pale brown, slender, hairless, ending in a spine

LEAVES
Alternate, 2½–4in, elliptical, pointed at tip, double-toothed, dark green above, paler below

FLOWERS
Appearing before the leaves, in clusters of usually 2–5, petals 5, rounded, white, to 1in

FRUITS
Up to 1in, red plum

ROSE FAMILY, ROSACEAE

Bitter Cherry
Prunus emarginata

Deciduous
Up to 30ft

J	F	M	A	M	J
J	A	S	O	N	D

ID FACT FILE

CROWN
Rounded

BARK
Dark reddish-brown, with horizontal lenticels, peeling horizontally

TWIGS
Reddish-brown, hairy when young

LEAVES
Alternate, 1–2in, elliptical, rounded at tip, finely toothed, dark green above, paler below

FLOWERS
Appearing with the leaves, in clusters of up to 10, petals 5, rounded, white, to ⅜in

FRUITS
Up to ⅜in, red cherry

Bitter Cherry is a common tree of the western states found south from Canada, through Montana and Washington, south to southern California and New Mexico in a variety of habitats. It is a small, fast-growing tree that is sometimes grown ornamentally. As the common name suggests, the fruit is bitter and unpalatable although it is used in jams and preserves. The bark and roots were previously used for medicinal qualities and the peeling bark was also utilized for basket weaving.

ROSE FAMILY, ROSACEAE

Evergreen
Up to 30ft

| J | F | M | A | M | J |
| J | A | S | O | N | D |

Hollyleaf Cherry
Prunus ilicifolia

ID FACT FILE

CROWN
Rounded

BARK
Reddish-brown,
fissured

TWIGS
Reddish-brown

LEAVES
Alternate, 1–2in,
elliptical, pointed
at tip, sharply
toothed, glossy
green above,
paler below

FLOWERS
Appearing with
the leaves, in
small clusters,
petals 5,
rounded, white,
to ¼in, fragrant

FRUITS
Up to ⅝in, red or
yellow plum

Restricted to the Pacific Coast of central and
southern California, Hollyleaf Cherry is
unusual in the genus for its evergreen leaves. It
is usually found alongside streams or on other
moist ground, although it is also found on dry
slopes in foothills, where it is more likely to be
shrublike. It has a long association with people,
being used as an ornamental and hedging plant
for many centuries in the western states. The
leaves, bark and roots were all also formerly
used for medicinal properties.

ROSE FAMILY, ROSACEAE

Deciduous
Up to 30ft

J	F	M	A	M	J
J	A	S	O	N	D

Mahaleb Cherry
Prunus mahaleb

ID FACT FILE

CROWN
Open, spreading

BARK
Gray-brown,
fissured and
ridged

TWIGS
Brown, hairy
when young

LEAVES
Alternate, 1–2in,
elliptical, pointed
at tip, sharply
toothed, green
above, paler and
hairy below

FLOWERS
Appearing with
the leaves, in
clusters of up to
10, petals 5,
rounded, white,
to ⅜in, fragrant

FRUITS
Up to ½in, black
cherry

Native to western Asia, and eastern to central
Europe, and introduced to the United States,
Mahaleb Cherry is grown across northwest and
northeast America. It has a vigorous rootstock
and is generally free of pests and diseases.
Consequently, it has been widely used as a
grafting tree for other species of cherry. The
seed kernels are edible and widely used in food
production in its native range.

ROSE FAMILY, ROSACEAE

Deciduous
Up to 30ft

| J | F | M | A | M | J |
| J | A | S | O | N | D |

Peach
Prunus persica

ID FACT FILE

CROWN
Rounded,
spreading

BARK
Gray-brown,
smooth with
horizontal
lenticels,
becoming scaly

TWIGS
Green, becoming
reddish-brown

LEAVES
Alternate, 3–6in,
lance-shaped,
finely toothed,
green above,
paler below

FLOWERS
Appearing before
the leaves,
solitary but close
together giving
the appearance
of clusters,
petals 5,
rounded, pink, to
1¼in

FRUITS
Up to 3¼in,
yellow and red,
rounded, hairy,
peach

This species, cultivated from ancient times,
was introduced to the United States by Spanish
colonists although it originates from China.
There are many cultivated varieties, both
ornamental and fruiting, and it is now so
widely grown that it has become naturalized in
parts of western and eastern North America. It
is, however, in common with other cultivated
trees of the genus, subject to a range of pests
and diseases.

ROSE FAMILY, ROSACEAE

Deciduous
Up to 100ft

J	F	M	A	M	J
J	A	S	O	N	D

Black Cherry
Prunus serotina

The most important of the native cherries to the United States, the Black Cherry has a variety of uses. It is widely distributed throughout the eastern states and as far west as Texas in the south and Minnesota in the north. There are, however, several geographic varieties found as far west as New Mexico and Arizona. The timber, mostly harvested commercially in the eastern part of the range, is a fine-grained wood used in cabinet-making and furniture. The fruit is also harvested and the bark has medicinal properties.

ID FACT FILE

CROWN
Oval, spreading

BARK
Gray, smooth, becoming dark-gray and fissured

TWIGS
Reddish-brown, slender, hairless

LEAVES
Alternate, 2–6in, elliptical, tapering, finely toothed, shiny-green above, paler and often hairy below

FLOWERS
Appearing after the leaves, in spikelike clusters up to 6in, petals 5, rounded, white, to ½in

FRUITS
Up to ½in, dark-red turning black, cherry

ROSE FAMILY, ROSACEAE

Deciduous
Up to 20ft

J	F	M	A	M	J
J	A	S	O	N	D

Common Chokecherry
Prunus virginiana

ID FACT FILE

CROWN
Narrow

BARK
Gray-brown,
smooth,
becoming scaly

TWIGS
Reddish-brown

LEAVES
Alternate,
1½–3in, elliptical,
pointed at tip,
finely toothed,
shiny green
above, paler
below, turning
yellow in autumn

FLOWERS
Appearing with
the leaves, in
small clusters,
petals 5,
rounded, white,
to ⅜in, fragrant

FRUITS
Up to ½in, red or
black cherry

An extremely widespread species, Common Chokecherry is found across the United States as far south as southern California, northern Texas, and North Carolina. It is also widely distributed throughout southern Canada. It is generally a colonizing species, which in turn becomes replaced by more shade-tolerant species. The fruit was formerly widely used in preserves and the leaves were also used for medicinal properties. It is a significant winter forage food for large animals, and in cultivation the tree is generally grown for the colorful fruits, although it is also grown ornamentally for the fragrant flowers, and as a windbreak.

ROSE FAMILY, ROSACEAE

Deciduous
Up to 40ft

J	F	M	A	M	J
J	A	S	O	N	D

European Mountain Ash
Sorbus aucuparia

ID FACT FILE

CROWN
Open, spreading

BARK
Gray, smooth, sometimes becoming ridged with age

TWIGS
Brown, hairy when young

LEAVES
Alternate, compound, pinnate, leaflets paired (except at apex), 11–17, up to 2in, lanceolate, toothed, green, whitish-hairy below, turning red in autumn

FLOWERS
Up to ½in, cream, in dense flat clusters up to 6in

FRUITS
Less than ½in berrylike, bright red, persistent

Native to wide areas of Europe, this species was most likely introduced to North America during Colonial times. Widely grown as an ornamental on account of the attractive bright red fruits (which are also extremely attractive to birdlife), the species has escaped from cultivation and is now naturalized across southern Canada to Alaska, and also across the northern United States. Often planted as a street tree, it naturally favors well-drained open sites and woodlands, often occurring in mountain sites giving the species its common name.

PEA FAMILY, FABACEAE

Deciduous
Up to 20ft

J	F	M	A	M	J
J	A	S	O	N	D

Sweet Acacia
Acacia farnesiana

Of unknown origin (although most likely tropical North or South America), Huisache—or Sweet Acacia as it is also known—is today widely-cultivated both within and outside the United States. Its native range may have extended as far north as southern Texas but it is today naturalized from Florida to southern California. It forms a small spiny tree that produces small, fragrant, yellow flowers in profusion in early spring.

ID FACT FILE

CROWN
Spreading

BARK
Gray, smooth, darkening with age

TWIGS
Brown, with lenticels and paired spines

LEAVES
Alternate, compound, bipinnate, up to 4in, 10–20 paired leaflets, elliptical, gray-green

FLOWERS
Up to ¼in, petals yellow, in small ball-like clusters, fragrant

FRUITS
1½–3¼in, cylindrical, segmented pod, brown, persistent

Deciduous
Up to 40ft

J	F	M	A	M	J
J	A	S	O	N	D

PEA FAMILY, FABACEAE

Eastern Redbud
Cercis canadensis

ID FACT FILE

CROWN
Spreading,
somewhat
rounded

BARK
Gray-brown,
becoming
furrowed

TWIGS
Brown, angled,
hairless

LEAVES
Alternate, 2½–5in,
heart-shaped,
pointed at apex,
petiole swollen,
mid-green above,
paler below,
turning yellow in
autumn

FLOWERS
Appearing before
the leaves,
pealike, up to
½in, petals pink,
in clusters along
branches and
twigs

FRUITS
2½–3in, flattened
pod, pink
maturing dark
brown, with flat,
elliptical brown
seeds within

This attractive ornamental tree is native to the
central eastern states, from New Jersey to
Nebraska in the north, and central Florida
to Texas in the south. It is also widely planted
in western North America for the bright pink
flowers that emerge before the leaves, making
this species especially striking. As with other
members of the genus, the flowers are edible
and the petals add sweetness to salads.

PEA FAMILY, FABACEAE

Evergreen
Up to 30ft

J	F	M	A	M	J
J	A	S	O	N	D

Desert Ironwood
Olneya tesota

ID FACT FILE

CROWN
Densely spreading to rounded

BARK
Gray, smooth, becoming fissured and shredding

TWIGS
Green, hairy when young, spiny

LEAVES
Alternate, pinnate, leaflets 4–8, up to ¾in, oval, leathery, green, hairy

FLOWERS
Up to ½in, pealike, white to pink, in small arched clusters, fragrant

FRUITS
Up to 2½in, cylindrical pod, brown, hairy, with shiny brown seeds

Known only from the Sonoran Desert of the southwest United States, where it is found growing along valleys at lower elevations, Tesota (the only species of its genus) is an important tree for a variety of reasons. Slow-growing and long-lived (to 1,500 years), it provides cover and food for a wide variety of fauna. It also has a profound impact on its own habitat by providing shade and protection in an otherwise harsh, exposed landscape, and like other legumes has the ability to fix nitrogen in the soil, encouraging a wide range of other flora to grow in close proximity. The heavy dense wood has been used for carving although the tree is becoming increasingly threatened in the wild.

PEA FAMILY, FABACEAE

Evergreen
Up to 40ft

| J | F | M | A | M | J |
| J | A | S | O | N | D |

Mexican Paloverde
Parkinsonia aculeata

ID FACT FILE

CROWN
Open, spreading

BARK
Yellow-green,
smooth,
becoming gray
and scaly

TWIGS
Yellow-green,
with long
unbranched
spines, often in
pairs or 3's

LEAVES
Alternate,
bipinnate, with
many leaflets up
to ¼in, oblong,
gray-green

FLOWERS
Up to ¾in,
pealike, petals 5,
yellow, largest
petal reddish, in
erect clusters

FRUITS
Up to 4in long,
segmented pod,
pointed, gray-
brown

This small spiny tree is native to desert grasslands of southwest United States and adjoining areas of Mexico and farther south. It has adapted to the arid conditions found in the southwest, often dropping its leaves in times of severe drought. In the United States it occurs naturally in the Trans Pecos range of Texas and there are also localized populations in southern Arizona, possibly introduced. It is, however, widely planted in the southwest as an ornamental tree and has become naturalized in many areas, in some cases to the extent of becoming a weed. The seeds were formerly dried and used as a food source.

PEA FAMILY, FABACEAE

Yellow Paloverde
Parkinsonia microphylla

Deciduous
Up to 27ft

J	F	M	A	M	J
J	A	S	O	N	D

ID FACT FILE

CROWN
Open

BARK
Green, smooth

TWIGS
Green, short,
spiny

LEAVES
Alternate,
compound,
bipinnate, up to
1in, 3–7 paired
leaflets,
elliptical, yellow-
green

FLOWERS
Up to ⅜in, petals
yellow or cream,
in small clusters,
in years with
sufficient rainfall

FRUITS
1½–3⅛in,
cylindrical,
segmented pod,
with 1–5 seeds,
brown, persistent

This remarkable small tree is native to the
Sonoran Desert of southwestern United Sates.
It is largely leafless for much of the year,
especially during hot dry periods as an
adaptation to reduce water loss through
transpiration. The lack of leaves is made up for
by chlorophyll being present in the twigs and
branches (giving the species its characteristic
green hue), and allowing it to photosynthesize
in a leafless state. It is also able to shed
branches and reduce in size during especially
harsh periods.

PEA FAMILY, FABACEAE

Deciduous
Up to 20ft

J	F	M	A	M	J
J	A	S	O	N	D

Honey Mesquite
Prosopis glandulosa

ID FACT FILE

CROWN
Open, spreading

BARK
Brown, thick, peeling in fibrous strips

TWIGS
Pale brown, with yellowish spines in pairs

LEAVES
Alternate, compound, bipinnate, usually with paired side shoots, leaflets 10–16, up to 1¼in, oblong to lanceolate, green

FLOWERS
Tiny, yellow, in dense clusters up to 3in

FRUITS
Up to 8in, narrowly cylindrical pod, brown, with many edible beanlike seeds

The most widespread and most eastern of the mesquite species, *Prosopis glandulosa* is found naturally in Oklahoma and Texas, although it is possibly naturalized farther north. Its range also extends westward to Utah and southern California. The species has long been used as a food source and as a fuel wood and also for the high-quality honey—bees are attracted to the fragrant yellow flowers. Naturally found in sandy soils, the species is tolerant of drought and may also be found growing in desert grasslands.

PEA FAMILY, FABACEAE

Deciduous
Up to 30ft

| J | F | M | A | M | J |
| J | A | S | O | N | D |

Screwbean Mesquite
Prosopis pubescens

ID FACT FILE

CROWN
Open, spreading

BARK
Gray-brown,
peeling in fibrous
strips

TWIGS
Pale brown,
densely hairy
when young, with
whitish spines in
pairs

LEAVES
Alternate,
compound,
bipinnate, usually
with paired side
shoots, leaflets
10–16, up to ½in,
pointed, green,
hairy

FLOWERS
Tiny, yellow, in
dense clusters
up to 2in

FRUITS
Up to 2in, coiled,
screwlike pod,
brown, in
clusters, with
many edible,
beanlike seeds

A distinctive tree found in the Trans Pecos range in Texas west to southern Utah and southern California (and south to Mexico), Screwbean Mesquite is easily recognized by the long, screwlike fruits (which are edible). Found alongside streams in desert valleys, it is only ever a small tree and may even be somewhat shrubby and thicket-forming. The fruits were previously an important food source and the bark was also exploited for medicinal uses. It is also sometimes planted as a street or garden tree for the curious fruits and peeling bark.

PEA FAMILY, FABACEAE

Deciduous
Up to 80ft

| J | F | M | A | M | J |
| J | A | S | O | N | D |

Black Locust
Robinia pseudoacacia

ID FACT FILE

CROWN
Open

BARK
Gray, furrowed
into forking
ridges

TWIGS
Brown, with
paired spines at
nodes

LEAVES
Alternate,
pinnate, usually
7–19 leaflets in
pairs except at
tip, each 1–2in,
elliptical, bristle-
tipped, toothed,
blue-green
above, paler
below

FLOWERS
Pea-shaped,
white, fragrant,
in drooping
clusters to 8in

FRUITS
2–4in, flattened
pod, brown

Black Locust is naturally found in the
Appalachian Mountains from Pennsylvania
south to Alabama, and also in the Ozarks from
Missouri to Oklahoma, but also now widely
naturalized across the United States. It grows
quickly and also spreads by suckers; older trees
may produce several trunks. The tree is widely
grown ornamentally and is also used for
erosion control. The durable wood is useful for
fenceposts and also makes a good firewood,
whilst the tree itself provides shelter and
forage for a range of birds. Several cultivars are
commercially available across the United
States and Europe.

DOGWOOD FAMILY, CORNACEAE

Pacific Dogwood
Cornus nuttalii

This widely grown ornamental tree with shock-resistant wood is used in a similar way to that of Flowering Dogwood (*C. florida*), notably for the heads of golf clubs. It is naturally found in a narrow coastal strip from Washington at low elevations, to southern California, where it can be found growing as high as 6,000ft. As with its eastern relative, *C. florida*, it is admired for its heads of showy flowers and clusters of bright red fruits.

Deciduous
Up to 60ft

J	F	M	A	M	J
J	A	S	O	N	D

ID FACT FILE

CROWN
Conical to rounded, with horizontal branches

BARK
Gray, becoming reddish-brown, and fissured into plates

TWIGS
Greenish, slender, hairy when young

LEAVES
Opposite, 2½–4½in, elliptical, wavy-edged, green above, paler and densely hairy below, turning orange and red in autumn

FLOWERS
Up to ¼in, yellowish, in dense clusters up to 1in, surrounded by 6 large, white, petal-like bracts

FRUITS
Up to ½in, berrylike, red, in clusters

SILK TASSLE FAMILY, GARRYACEAE

Evergreen
Up to 20ft

J	F	M	A	M	J
J	A	S	O	N	D

Wavyleaf Silktassle

Garrya elliptica

This species is the only member of this small genus that is a tree, all other species being shrubs. It is found on rocky soils in evergreen forests from Oregon to southern California. Formerly placed in the family Cornaceae, the genus *Garrya* is now considered distinct enough to merit its own family status, Garryaceae. Wavyleaf Silktassle is a widely grown and attractive ornamental tree, especially male plants when in flower. The bark was also formerly used medicinally.

ID FACT FILE

CROWN
Irregular, spreading

BARK
Greenish, smooth, becoming gray and fissured

TWIGS
Greenish-brown, angled, hairy when young

LEAVES
Opposite, 2–3in, elliptical, somewhat leathery, wavy-edged, shiny green above, gray and densely hairy below

FLOWERS
Tiny, scaly, and without petals, Greenish-yellow, in pendent catkinlike clusters up to 5in, males and females on separate plants, male catkins longer

FRUITS
Up to ½in, rounded, berrylike, purple, hairy

BUCKTHORN FAMILY, RHAMNACEAE

Evergreen
Up to 20ft

J	F	M	A	M	J
J	A	S	O	N	D

Blueblossom
Ceanothus thyrsiflorus

Native to the Pacific Coast of Oregon and
California, Blueblossom is a striking plant with
dense clusters of blue, lilaclike flowers, found
in a variety of habitats from forest to scrub and
prairie lands. It is the largest member of the
genus and the only one that attains treelike
proportions, although this variable species can
also be found growing as a shrub in places.
The dense fragrant blooms have a cleaning,
soaplike property when rubbed.

ID FACT FILE

CROWN
Dense,
spreading

BARK
Reddish-brown,
fissured

TWIGS
Greenish, hairy
when young

LEAVES
Opposite,
elliptical to
rounded,
toothed, slightly
leathery, up to
2in, shiny green
above, paler and
slightly hairy
below

FLOWERS
Tiny, in dense
branched
clusters up to
3¼in, deep blue,
fragrant

FRUITS
Up to ¼in,
3-lobed capsule,
black

BUCKTHORN FAMILY, RHAMNACEAE

Deciduous
Up to 30ft

| J | F | M | A | M | J |
| J | A | S | O | N | D |

Cascara False Buckthorn
Frangula purshiana

ID FACT FILE

CROWN
Irregularly
rounded

BARK
Gray, smooth,
aromatic

TWIGS
Gray, hairy when
young

LEAVES
Opposite, 2½–7in,
oval, wavy-edged,
shiny green
above, paler and
sometimes hairy
below, turning
yellow in autumn

FLOWERS
Tiny, greenish-
yellow, bell-
shaped, in
clusters up to 50,
in axils of leaves

FRUITS
Up to ½in,
berrylike,
purplish-black

Cascara False Buckthorn is best known for the laxative drug Cascara, which is extracted from the bark. It has long been used for its medicinal properties, and the bark is harvested commercially. It is generally found on moist soils, either as a colonizing species or as an understory plant in coniferous and evergreen forests. On drier sites it tends to become more shrubby. Its native range is south from British Columbia south to northern California although it is also found sporadically in the Rocky Mountains of northern Idaho and Montana.

HORSE-CHESTNUT FAMILY, HIPPOCASTANACEAE

Deciduous
Up to 23ft

J	F	M	A	M	J
J	A	S	O	N	D

California Buckeye

Aesculus californica

ID FACT FILE

CROWN
Rounded

BARK
Gray, smooth

TWIGS
Reddish-brown, with sticky buds

LEAVES
Opposite, palmate, up to 6in long, with 5-toothed leaflets, green above, whitish below, turning yellow in autumn

FLOWERS
Appearing after the leaves, white, fragrant, in erect panicles up to 8in long

FRUITS
Up to 3in, brown, pear-shaped, spineless husk, containing usually, single brown seed

This species is adapted to a habitat prone to forest fires where it tends to be thicket forming, regenerating from burned stumps. Native to the southern Cascades and Coastal Ranges of California and the Sierra Nevada mountains, it is a small tree when not affected by fire. All parts of the plants are poisonous although the seeds were previously used as a foodstuff after leaching. The untreated seeds were also used as a fish poison, stunning them so they were easily caught. The tree tends to become deciduous early in drier areas, such as the Sierra Nevada mountains, shedding its leaves in summer if sufficient moisture is not available. It is a relatively fast-growing and long-lived tree and attractive when mature.

HORSE-CHESTNUT FAMILY, HIPPOCASTANACEAE

Deciduous
Up to 120ft

J	F	M	A	M	J
J	A	S	O	N	D

Horse Chestnut

Aesculus hippocastanum

This large tree is native to southeastern Europe but introduced across the United States, where it has escaped into the wild in the northeast. Planted as a shade and ornamental or street tree, it bears attractive panicles of white flowers in the spring. This species also produces the spiny fruits containing the seed sometimes referred to as "conkers."

ID FACT FILE

CROWN
Spreading, elliptical

BARK
Gray-brown, smooth, becoming fissured and scaly with age

TWIGS
Red-brown, smooth with large dark brown sticky winter buds

LEAVES
Opposite, palmate, 5–7 toothed leaflets up to 10in long, dark green above, paler below

FLOWERS
¾in across, 4–5 spreading petals, white spotted red and yellow at base with stamens protruding, held in erect branched panicles up to 10in

FRUIT
Up to 2½in, green ripening brown, husk spiny, enclosing shiny brown seed

MAPLE FAMILY, ACERACEAE

Deciduous
Up to 33ft

J	F	M	A	M	J
J	A	S	O	N	D

Rocky Mountain Maple
Acer glabrum

ID FACT FILE

CROWN
Irregular

BARK
Gray, smooth

TWIGS
Reddish-brown,
slender

LEAVES
Opposite, 2–5in,
3-lobed, each
lobe pointed,
toothed, lobes
sometimes
becoming
leaflets, shiny-
green above,
paler below,
turning red and
yellow in autumn

FLOWERS
Appearing with
the leaves,
greenish-yellow,
in branched
clusters, males
and females on
separate trees

FRUITS
Paired, reddish-
brown, long-
winged, forming
a fork, 1in long

Rock Maple is a moisture-loving species found alongside rivers and streams in the mountains of the northwest. It ranges from southeast Alaska south to California and is also found in the Rockies south to New Mexico. It is the northernmost species of maple in the New World. It is fairly insignificant for most of the year but the foliage develops attractive autumn color.

Deciduous
Up to 40ft

Canyon Maple
Acer grandidentatum

As suggested by the common name, this species is usually found in moist sites in canyons on the western slopes of the Rockies from Idaho to Arizona, and also New Mexico to Texas. It is related to the eastern Sugar Maple (*Acer saccharum*) and is exploited for its sap, which is used for maple sugar in the same way. It is occasionally grown as an ornamental specimen for the red and yellow autumn color.

ID FACT FILE

CROWN
Rounded, spreading

BARK
Gray-brown, smooth

TWIGS
Reddish-brown, slender

LEAVES
Opposite, 2–3¼in, 5-lobed, basal lobes small, shiny-green above, paler and hairy below, turning red and yellow in autumn

FLOWERS
Appearing with the leaves, yellow, in branched, pendent clusters, males and females occurring together or separately on same tree

FRUITS
Paired, red, long-winged, forming a fork, 1¼in long

MAPLE FAMILY, ACERACEAE

Deciduous
Up to 80ft

| J | F | M | A | M | J |
| J | A | S | O | N | D |

Bigleaf Maple
Acer macrophyllum

ID FACT FILE

CROWN
Narrow to broadly rounded

BARK
Brown, furrowed

TWIGS
Greenish, hairless

LEAVES
Opposite, 6–12in, deeply 5-lobed, lobes pointed and themselves lobed or slightly toothed, shiny-green above, paler and hairy below, turning orange and yellow in autumn

FLOWERS
Appearing usually after the leaves, yellow, in narrow, pendent clusters, males and females occurring together

FRUITS
Paired, brown, long-winged, forming a fork, 1½in long, hairy

Bigleaf Maple is a variable long-lived species, potentially growing to a large tree with distinctive large leaves up to 12in across, from which both the scientific and common names derive. It is native to the Pacific northwest coast, where it favors streamside locations in the mountain ranges. Although sometimes grown ornamentally on account of its autumn foliage, it is not overly common in cultivation. The timber, however, is harvested commercially.

MAPLE FAMILY, ACERACEAE

Deciduous
Up to 65ft

| J | F | M | A | M | J |
| J | A | S | O | N | D |

Box Elder
Acer negundo

This common, fast-growing, short-lived tree is distributed throughout the Great Plains and as far south as Florida, with scattered populations through to California. Uniquely amongst the maples this species has pinnately compound as opposed to palmately simple leaves making it easily identifiable. Naturally found along lakeshores and riverbanks, it readily colonizes disturbed sites and a variegated form is often grown ornamentally.

ID FACT FILE

CROWN
Irregular

BARK
Gray-brown, smooth becoming fissured

TWIGS
Green, developing a gray-white bloom in late summer, becoming purple, slender, hairless

LEAVES
Opposite, 4–6in, pinnate with 5–7 toothed, sometimes lobed leaflets, pale green mostly hairless, turning yellow in autumn

FLOWERS
Appearing before leaves, males with red anthers, females greenish-yellow and insignificant on different trees; petals absent

FRUITS
Paired, brown, winged, ⅜in long, persistent

CASHEW FAMILY, ANACARDIACEAE

Deciduous
Up to 20ft

J	F	M	A	M	J
J	A	S	O	N	D

Smooth Sumac

Rhus glabra

ID FACT FILE

CROWN
Irregular,
spreading

BARK
Gray-brown,
smooth,
becoming scaly
with age

TWIGS
Gray, smooth,
with whitish
bloom and small,
rounded, hairy
buds

LEAVES
Alternate,
compound,
pinnate, leaflets
11–31, leaflets
lanceolate,
2½–5in, toothed,
dark green above,
paler and hairy
below, turning red
in autumn

FLOWERS
Tiny, yellow-
white, in dense
erect clusters up
to 8in, males
and females on
separate trees

FRUITS
Up to ⅛in,
rounded,
reddish, in dense
erect clusters

Smooth Sumac is the most widespread tree in
the United States, native to all 48 contiguous
states. The main center of distribution is in the
east, although it is absent from the Mississippi
delta and sporadic along the Gulf Coast. In the
west it is largely restricted to montane habitats in
the Rockies, where it grows at a higher altitude.
It is typically thicket or colony forming and may
also be shrublike. It is an attractive small tree
with good autumn color, and there are several
cultivated, ornamental forms.

CASHEW FAMILY, ANACARDIACEAE

Evergreen
Up to 16ft

J	F	M	A	M	J
J	A	S	O	N	D

Sugar Sumac
Rhus ovata

ID FACT FILE

CROWN
Spreading

BARK
Gray-brown,
smooth,
becoming scaly
with age

TWIGS
Reddish-green,
smooth, with
small hairy buds

LEAVES
Simple, alternate,
oval, 1½–4in,
leathery, pointed
at apex, shiny
green above,
paler below,
fragrant,
evergreen

FLOWERS
Tiny, pinkish-
white, in dense
erect clusters up
to 2in, males
and females on
separate plants

FRUITS
Up to ¼in,
elliptical, reddish,
hairy, in dense
erect clusters,
persistent

A common sumac of rocky, mountain slopes in California and Arizona, extending south to the Baja Peninsula, this species is extremely tolerant of drought and may be either a shrub, or a small tree. It is a useful ornamental plant in especially harsh areas where little else will tolerate full sun conditions and little moisture. Birds find the clusters of red fruits attractive in the summer. The sweetish pulp surrounding the seed was previously used as a sweetener.

CITRUS FAMILY, RUTACEAE

Deciduous
Up to 20ft

J	F	M	A	M	J
J	A	S	O	N	D

Hop Tree
Ptelea trifoliata

ID FACT FILE

CROWN
Narrowly rounded

BARK
Gray-brown,
scaly, aromatic

TWIGS
Brown, hairy

LEAVES
Alternate,
compound,
palmate, leaflets
3, elliptical, up
to 3in, hairy
when young,
unpleasantly
aromatic, green
above, paler
below, turning
yellow in autumn

FLOWERS
Up to ½in, in
terminal clusters,
greenish-white

FRUITS
Up to 1in, disk-
shaped, with
papery wing,
ripening yellow-
brown, in
pendent clusters

Hop Tree has an extensive and wide distribution, albeit scattered. It is found from New York south to Florida and west to Texas, from where it spreads north to the Great Lakes area and Wisconsin. In addition, other isolated populations are known in Arizona and Utah. Probably as a result of such a scattered distribution, there are many natural varieties and forms and it also occurs as a shrub in places. The common name relates to the fact that the bitter fruits were previously used to brew beer.

OLIVE FAMILY, OLEACEAE

Oregon Ash
Fraxinus latifolia

Deciduous
Up to 50ft

ID FACT FILE

CROWN
Narrow, dense

BARK
Gray-brown,
thickly furrowed
and ridged

TWIGS
Greenish-brown,
hairy

LEAVES
Opposite,
pinnate, leaflets
5–9, each 2–5in,
elliptical,
sometimes
slightly toothed,
green above,
paler and hairy
below

FLOWERS
Appearing before
the leaves, tiny,
yellow-green, in
dense clusters,
males and
females on
separate trees

FRUITS
1¼–2in long, pale
brown, broadly
winged, in
pendent clusters

Oregon Ash is the only species of the genus native to the northwestern United States. A tree of wetland habitats and seasonally flooded areas, it is native to Washington, Oregon, and California along the Coastal Ranges and Sierra Nevada mountains. Although it tends to be shrublike when young, it matures into a handsome single-stemmed tree and is often grown as an ornamental specimen. As with other wetland ash species, it is utilized in wetland restoration, and the wood is also used for furniture and flooring.

OLIVE FAMILY, OLEACEAE

Deciduous
Up to 40ft

| J | F | M | A | M | J |
| J | A | S | O | N | D |

Arizona Ash
Fraxinus velutina

A common street tree of the southwest (from Texas to California, and Nevada to Utah), Arizona Ash is adapted to the arid climate in which it grows in scattered populations. It is a riparian tree, growing in moist gullies along the bottoms of canyons. Its leaves are densely hairy and slightly thickened, which helps the tree stay cool by reducing water loss.

ID FACT FILE

CROWN
Open, spreading

BARK
Gray-brown, furrowed into diamondlike ridges

TWIGS
Gray-brown, hairy

LEAVES
Opposite, pinnate, leaflets 5–9, each 1¼–3in, lance-shaped, wavy to slightly toothed, thickened, green above, paler and densely hairy below, turning yellow in autumn

FLOWERS
Appearing before the leaves, tiny, yellow-green, in dense clusters, males and females on separate trees

FRUITS
1in long, pale brown, narrowly winged, in pendent clusters

FIGWORT FAMILY, SCROPHULARIACEAE

Deciduous
Up to 80ft

| J | F | M | A | M | J |
| J | A | S | O | N | D |

Princess Tree
Paulownia tomentosa

ID FACT FILE

CROWN
Broad, open,
with spreading
branches

BARK
Gray-brown,
shallowly
fissured

TWIGS
Brown, densely
hairy when young

LEAVES
Opposite, up to
18in, heart-
shaped,
sometimes 3-
lobed, with long,
pointed tip, pale
green and hairy
above, densely
gray-hairy below

FLOWERS
2½in long,
tubular, with 5
spreading,
unequal lobes,
violet, in erect
clusters 6–12in

FRUITS
Up to 2in, ovoid,
pointed at end,
glossy greenish-
brown, podlike

The Princess Tree is a native of China but has been introduced as a widely grown ornamental; it is naturalized in many states where it is found in open areas. The foxglovelike flowers are conspicuous, appearing before the leaves and are bright violet in color on the outside and yellow inside. The flowers are actually formed in the autumn of the previous year, remaining dormant as hairy brown buds over winter.

BIGNONIA FAMILY, BIGNONIACEAE

Deciduous
Up to 65ft

J	F	M	A	M	J
J	A	S	O	N	D

Indian Bean Tree
Catalpa bignonioides

The Indian Bean Tree is native to the southeast of North America—most likely originating from the Alabama, Georgia, Mississippi, and Florida area—but now it is naturalized across the eastern states as far north as New England and west to Texas. Elsewhere it is grown ornamentally. It has become so widely established because of its many attractive features—large leaves, showy flowers, and distinctive fruits—for which it is grown ornamentally. It also makes an attractive shade tree. Its popularity as a garden plant has unsurprisingly given rise to the development of many cultivated varieties, and both these and the species itself are widely grown within and outside the United States.

ID FACT FILE

CROWN
Broad, domed

BARK
Brownish-gray, smooth, becoming scaly

TWIGS
Smooth, thick, crooked, green becoming brown

LEAVES
Opposite or in whorls of 3, ovate, pointed at tip and heart-shaped at base, 4–10in, dull green above, paler and hairy below

FLOWERS
Showy, in erect branched clusters up to 10in, bell-shaped, 5 fringed petals, white, spotted yellow and purple, with 2 orange lines on the inside, up to 2in across

FRUITS
Up to 12in long and ½in wide, beanlike pod, pendulous, brown, persisting on tree through winter

BIGNONIA FAMILY, BIGNONIACEAE

Deciduous
Up to 80ft

J	F	M	A	M	J
J	A	S	O	N	D

Northern Catalpa
Catalpa speciosa

ID FACT FILE

CROWN
Broad, spreading

BARK
Brownish-gray,
smooth
becoming scaly

TWIGS
Smooth, thick,
crooked, green
becoming brown

LEAVES
Opposite or in
whorls of 3,
ovate, pointed at
tip and heart-
shaped at base,
6–12in, dull
green above,
paler and hairy
below

FLOWERS
Showy, in erect
branched
clusters up to
8in, bell-shaped,
5 fringed petals,
white, spotted
yellow and
purple, with 2
orange lines on
the inside, up to
2½in across

FRUITS
Up to 16in long
and ⅝in wide,
beanlike pod,
pendulous,
brown, persisting
on tree through
winter

Very similar to its southern relative *C. bignonioides*, Northern Catalpa is also of unknown definite origin, although the likely original range is thought to be the Indiana, Arkansas region. This species is now widely naturalized throughout eastern North America, and grown ornamentally elsewhere. It is slightly larger with larger flowers than its southern relative but otherwise virtually identical.

BIGNONIA FAMILY, BIGNONIACEAE

Deciduous
Up to 27ft

| J | F | M | A | M | J |
| J | A | S | O | N | D |

Desert Willow
Chilopsis linearis

ID FACT FILE

CROWN
Open, spreading

BARK
Dark brown,
scaly and
furrowed

TWIGS
Brown, slender

LEAVES
Opposite,
sometimes
alternate, linear-
lanceolate,
3–6in, pale green

FLOWERS
Up to 1¼in,
funnel-shaped
with 5 unequal
lobes, white
tinged pink,
woolly, in terminal
clusters up to 4in

FRUITS
Up to 8in,
cylindrical
capsule, brown,
persistent, with
many winged
seeds

Native to the extreme southwest of the United States, from southern California to Texas, this species (despite the common name) is unrelated to willows but is so named for the willowlike leaves. Usually found growing in moist areas, Desert Willow is an important species for erosion control and soil stabilization. It also has a variety of medicinal properties, the flowers, leaves and bark all being potentially useful although it has not been extensively used for this purpose.

MADDER FAMILY, RUBIACEAE

Deciduous
Up to 20ft

J	F	M	A	M	J
J	A	S	O	N	D

Buttonbush
Cephalanthus occidentalis

ID FACT FILE

CROWN
Open, spreading

BARK
Gray-brown with
vertical lenticels,
becoming
reddish-brown
and fissured

TWIGS
Reddish-brown,
hairless

LEAVES
Opposite or in
whorls of 3,
2½–6in, elliptical,
pointed at apex,
shiny green
above, paler
below

FLOWERS
Tubular, up to
⅜in, petals white,
style long and
protruding,
fragrant, in erect
ball-like clusters

FRUITS
Up to 1in,
globular, brown,
with many
2-seeded nutlets

Buttonbush is a small tree native to the eastern states from Minnesota and Maine in the south to Texas and Florida in the south. With scattered populations also found in Arizona and California. This ungainly, much-branched species is generally shrublike in the northern part of its range, becoming treelike in the south, where the foliage also becomes semi-evergreen. It favors wetland sites, where aquatic birds feed on the seeds. The foliage, however, is poisonous although the bark was previously purported to have medicinal properties.

PALM FAMILY, ARECACEAE

Evergreen
Up to 60ft

J	F	M	A	M	J
J	A	S	O	N	D

Fanpalm
Washingtonia filifera

This distinctive fan palm is native to the deserts, gorges and canyons of southern California and Arizona, and also Mexico. It is a large tree with large fibrous leaves, which characteristically clothe the trunk as they die off as the tree grows, giving the tree its alternative name, "Petticoat Palm." It is the only native western palm species and while uncommon in the wild, it is widely grown as a street tree. The fruits and seeds were formerly much harvested.

ID FACT FILE

CROWN
Rounded

BARK
Gray

LEAVES
Alternate, compound, palmate, 3–6ft, fan-shaped, segments pointed, fibrous, drooping, coarse, gray-green

FLOWERS
Tiny, white, in large, branched, drooping clusters up to 13ft

FRUITS
Up to ½in, berrylike, black, in large branched clusters

AGAVE FAMILY, AGAVACEAE

Evergreen
Up to 60ft

Joshua Tree
Yucca brevifolia

ID FACT FILE

CROWN
Broad, many
individual crowns

BARK
Pale brown,
becoming
furrowed and
ridged

LEAVES
Alternate, in
clusters at the
ends of the
branches,
8–16in, sword-
shaped, sharp
pointed, toothed,
stiff, blue-green

FLOWERS
Up to 1½in, bell-
shaped, yellow-
green, in large,
upright, branched
clusters up to
18in at the ends
of the branches

FRUITS
Up to 5in,
reddish-brown,
elliptical, six-
celled capsule

A native of the Mohave Desert and found from
California, to Nevada, Utah, and Arizona,
Joshua Tree is well adapted to the harsh dry
climate in which it lives. It is slow-growing and
able to withstand the freezing night
temperatures of the desert, although it is
intolerant of cool wet conditions. It is a
distinctive tree with successively forking
branches and dense clusters of swordlike
leaves, and is an important habitat tree,
exploited by a variety of birdlife.

AGAVE FAMILY, AGAVACEAE

Evergreen
Up to 20ft

J	F	M	A	M	J
J	A	S	O	N	D

Mohave Yucca
Yucca schidigera

ID FACT FILE

CROWN
Broad, many
individual crowns

BARK
Gray-brown,
becoming scaly
and rough

LEAVES
Alternate, in
clusters at the
ends of the
branches,
12–24in, sword-
shaped, thick,
sharp pointed,
fibrous, stiff,
blue-green

FLOWERS
Up to 1½in,
bell-shaped,
creamy-white,
sometimes
purple-tinged, in
large, upright,
branched
clusters up to
32in at the ends
of the branches

FRUITS
Up to 4in,
dark brown,
cylindrical,
6-celled capsule

Smaller than its better-known relative, the
Joshua Tree (*Y. brevifolia*), Mohave Yucca is
found in the same desert habitat across
California, Nevada, Utah, and Arizona. It also
extends into the Baja California Peninsula and
has a wider altitudinal range than its fellow
Yucca species. The fruits, which are high in
vitamins, were previously harvested and
various extracts of the plant are reported to
have medicinal properties.

INDEX

Abies amabilis 12
  bracteata 13
  concolor 14
  grandis 15
  lassiocarpa 16
  magnifica 17
  procera 18
Acacia farnesiana 153
Acacia, Sweet 153
Acer glabrum 169
  grandidentatum 170
  macrophyllum 171
  negundo 172
  saccharum 170
Aesculus californica 166
  hippocastanum 168
Alder, Arizona 112
  Mountain 115
  Red 114
  Speckled 111
  White 113
Alnus incana 111
  oblongifolia 112
  rhombifolia 113
  rubra 114
  tenuifolia 115
Amelanchier alnifolia 138
Apple, Cultivated 142
  Wild 143
Arbutus menziesii 134
  xalapensis 136
Ash, Arizona 178
  European Mountain 152
  Oregon 177
Aspen, Quaking 125

Bean Tree, Indian 180
Betula occidentalis 116
  papyrifera 117
Birch, Paper 117
  Water 116
Blueblossom 164
Buckeye, California 166
Buckthorn, Cascara False 165

Buttonbush 184

Calocedrus decurrens 55
Carya texana 90
Catalpa bignonioides 180
  speciosa 182
Catalpa, Northern 182
Ceanothus thyrsiflorus 164
Cedar, Alaska 57
  Incense 55
  Western Red 75
Celtis reticulata 88
Cephalanthus occidentalis 184
Cercis canadensis 154
Cereus giganteus 119
Chamaecyparis lawsoniana 56
  nootkatensis 57
Cherry, Bitter 145
  Black 149
  Hollyleaf 146
  Mahaleb 147
Chestnut, Horse 168
Chilopsis linearis 183
Chinkapin, Giant 96
Chokecherry, Common 150
Chrysolepis chrysophylla 96
Cornus florida 162
  nuttalii 162
Cottonwood, Eastern 124
  Fremont 124
  Narrowleaf 122
Crabapple, Western Oregon 141
Crataegus douglasii 139
  monogyna 140
  oxyacantha 140
Cupressus arizonica 58
  bakeri 59
  goveniana 60
  guadalupensis 61
  macnabii 64
  macrocarpa 62
  sargentii 64
Cypress, Arizona 58
  Baker 59

Gowan 60
Lawson 56
Macnab 64
Monterey 62
Sargent 64
Tecate 61

Dogwood, Flowering 162
Pacific 162

Elder, Box 172
Elm, American 89

Fanpalm 185
Fir, Alpine 16
Bigcone Douglas 51
Bristlecone 13
Californian Red 17
Douglas 52
Grand 15
Noble 18
Pacific Silver 12
White 14
Fraxinus latifolia 177
velutina 178

Garrya elliptica 163
Ginkgo 11
Ginkgo biloba 11

Hackberry, Netleaf 88
Hawthorn, Black 139
English 140
Oneseed 140
Hemlock, Mountain 54
Western 53
Hickory, Black 90
Hop Tree 176
Hophornbeam, Western 118

Ironwood, Desert 155

Joshua Tree 186
Juglans hindsii 92
major 93
microcarpa 94

Juniper, Alligator 67
California 65
Common 66
Oneseed 68
Rocky Mountain 72
Utah 70
Western 69
Juniperus californica 65
communis 66
deppeana 67
monosperma 68
occidentalis 69
osteosperma 70
scopulorum 72

Larch, Subalpine 20
Western 21
Larix lyalli 20
occidentalis 21
Laurel, Californian 81
Liquidambar styraciflua 84
Liriodendron tulipifera 78
Lithocarpus densiflorus 97
Locust, Black 160

Maclura pomifera 85
Madrone, Pacific 134
Texas 136
Magnolia grandiflora 80
Magnolia, Southern 80
Maidenhair Tree 11
Malus fusca 141
pumila 142
sylvestris 143
Maple, Bigleaf 171
Canyon 170
Rocky Mountain 169
Sugar 170
Mesquite, Honey 158
Screwbean 159
Morus alba 86
rubra 87
Mulberry, Red 87
White 86

Nutmeg, California 77

Oak, Arizona White 99
  Blue 101
  California 106
  Canyon Live 100
  Chinkapin 107
  Coast Live 98
  Coastal Sage Scrub 102
  Gambel 103
  Gray 99, 105
  Interior Live 110
  Oregon White 104
  Sandpaper 109
  Water 108
Olneya tesota 155
Orange, Osage 85
Ostrya knowltonii 118

Paloverde, Mexican 156
  Yellow 157
Parkinsonia aculeata 156
  microphylla 157
Paulownia tomentosa 179
Peach 148
Picea breweriana 22
  engelmannii 23
  glauca 24
  mariana 25
  pungens 26
  sitchensis 27
Pine, Apache 35
  Bishop 43
  Colorado 29
  Digger 47
  Intermountain Bristlecone 40
  Jeffrey 37
  Knobcone 30
  Limber 36
  Lodgepole 32
  Monterey 46
  Ponderosa 44
  Scots 49
  Shore 32
  Southwestern White 48
  Sugar 38
  Torrey 50
  Western White 42

  Whitebark 28
Pinus albicaulis 28
  aristata 29, 40
  attenuata 30
  cembroides 31
  contorta 32
  edulis 31, 34
  engelmanii 35
  flexilis 36
  jeffreyi 37
  lambertiana 38
  longaeva 40
  monophylla 41
  monticola 42
  muricata 43
  ponderosa 44
  quadrifolia 45
  radiata 46
  sabiniana 47
  strobiformis 48
  sylvestris 49
  torreyana 50
Pinyon 34
  Mexican 31
  Parry 45
  Singleleaf 41
Platanus racemosa 82
  wrightii 83
Plum, American 144
Poplar, Balsam 123
  White 120
Populus alba 120
  angustifolia 122
  balsamifera 123
  deltoides 124
  fremontii 124
  tremuloides 125
Princess Tree 179
Prosopis glandulosa 158
  pubescens 159
Prunus americana 144
  emarginata 145
  ilicifolia 146
  mahaleb 147
  persica 148
  serotina 149

virginiana 150
Pseudotsuga macrocarpa 51
  menziesii 52
Ptelea trifoliata 176

Quercus agrifolia 98
  arizonica 99, 105
  chrysolepis 100
  douglasii 101
  dumosa 102
  gambelii 103
  garryana 104
  grisea 99, 105
  lobata 106
  muehlenbergii 107
  nigra 108
  pungens 109
  wislizeni 110

Redbud, Eastern 154
Redwood 74
Rhamnus purshiana 165
Rhus glabra 173
  ovata 174
Robinia pseudoacacia 160

Saguaro 119
Salix alaxensis 126
  amygdaloides 127
  discolor 128
  exigua 130
  hindsiana 130
  lasiandra 131
  lasiolepis 132
  lucida 131
  nigra 133
Sequoia sempervirens 74
Sequoia, Giant 73
Sequoiadendron giganteum 73
Serviceberry, Saskatoon 138
Silktassle, Wavyleaf 163
Sorbus aucuparia 152

Spruce, Black 25
  Blue 26
  Brewer's Weeping 22
  Colorado 26
  Engelmann's 23
  Sitka 27
  White 24
Sumac, Smooth 173
  Sugar 174
Sweetgum 84
Sycamore, Arizona 83
  California 82

Tanoak 97
Taxus brevifolia 76
Thuja plicata 75
Torreya californica 77
Tsuga heterophylla 53
  mertensia 54
Tulip Tree 78

Ulmus americana 89
Umbellularia californica 81

Walnut, Arizona 93
  Little 94
  Northern California 92
Washingtonia filifera 185
Willow, Arroyo 132
  Black 133
  Desert 183
  Feltleaf 126
  Hinds 130
  Narrowleaf 130
  Pacific 131
  Peachleaf 127
  Pussy 128
  Shining 131

Yew, Western 76
Yucca brevifolia 186
  schidigera 187
Yucca, Mohave 187

PICTURE CREDITS

All artwork © David More, except for pp.11, 15, 22, 23, 26, 27, 46, 49, 66, 73, 74, 84, 111, 140, 143, 148, 149, 152, 172, 179 © Carol Merryman.

pp.11, 25, 66, 78, 80, 84, 95, 100, 108, 109, 111, 121, 123, 129, 140, 148, 149, 154, 161, 168, 172, 173, 176, 179, 181, 182, 184 © FLPA www.flpa-images.co.uk; pp.12, 110 © Nature Photographers/Andrew Cleave; pp.13, 24, 26, 83, 85, 87, 106, 122, 157, 159, 175 © Grant Heilman Photography, inc; pp.14, 28, 35, 41, 42, 55, 56, 57, 62, 73, 114, 116, 147, 162, 164, 167, 187 © Garden Picture Library; pp.15 © cfgphoto.com; pp.16, 19, 21, 23, 29, 32, 34, 40, 46, 49, 52, 53, 68, 71, 74, 76, 81, 101, 105, 117, 119, 124, 125, 133, 143, 144, 151, 152, 158, 171, 185, 186 © NHPA/Photoshot (www.nhpa.co.uk); pp.17, 22, 36, 39, 65, 69, 72, 77, 103, 107, 126, 130, 142, 170, 183 © Oxford Scientific Photo Library; pp.20, 27, 44, 75, 86, 169, 177 © Ben Legler; pp.22, 36, 39, 43, 65, 69, 72, 77, 103, 107, 126, 130, 142, 170, 183 © Oxford Scientific Photo Library; pp.59, 99, 139 © Albert Bussewitz/Mass Audubon Collection; pp.30, 45, 51, 54, 92, 145, 146 © Br. Alfred Brousseau, Saint Mary's College; pp.31, 48 © Martin Beebee photography; p37 © Dr. Lorence G. Collins; pp.43, 135 © Susan McDougall, USDA-NRCS PLANTS Database; pp.47, 58, 64, 97, 132, 153, 178 © Saxon Holt Photography; pp.50, 61, 67, 82, 98, 102, 156, 163 © www.naturalvisions.co.uk; pp.60, 112 © J.S. Peterson, USDA-NRCS PLANTS Database; pp.88, 118 © Al Schneider; p89 © Louis M. Landry; p91 © Samuel Roberts Noble Foundation, Inc.; p93 © Robert Potts, California Academy; p96 © Nature Photographers/Brinsley Burbidge; p105 © Robert Sivinski; p113 © Michael L. Charters; p127 © Robert H. Mohlenbrock, USDA-NRCS PLANTS Database; p131 © William and Wilma Follette, USDA-NRCS PLANTS Database; p137 © Ralph Arvesen; p138 © George Rembert; pp.141, 155 © Bruce Coleman Inc/FLPA; p152 © Dr Walter Obermayer; p165 © 1991 Dan Post.